Man of God
A Study of the Priesthood

Man of God

A Study of the Priesthood

Charles R. Meyer

DOUBLEDAY & COMPANY, INC., GARDEN CITY, NEW YORK
1974

ISBN: 0-385-01024-9
Library of Congress Catalog Card Number 73–10813

Contents

Contents

Man of God
A Study of the Priesthood

CHAPTER I
Priestly Life-style in the Past

The priesthood is in trouble. Membership in the Church may be increasing slightly year by year, but the number of priests in the active ministry is rapidly declining. Nor are there any good prospects of a significant abatement in the years to come. If anything, judged by purely human standards, the situation will worsen. More telling than the loss of those who are already priests is the drastic reduction in the number of seminarians. It augurs a marked penury of priests in the not too far distant future.

Various reasons have been set forth for the dearth of vocations. The clerical state is no longer as prestigious as it was in the past. The actions of some priests have cheapened the priestly calling in the eyes of many who in times past held it in the highest regard. In the ghetto communities of former days the well-educated priest often was regarded as a kind of hero. But ours is an era of mass education and Consciousness III. Men in the past were largely occupied with religion. The centering of today's concerns around science and technology has produced a tidal drift toward secularity. The priest is an agent of organized religion. What religious feelings remain in modern secularized society tend to be antithetical to established religions. Priesthood means celibacy. The value that the current culture sets not only upon sexual fulfillment but also upon personal intimacy and generativity is a counter-indicator of happiness in the priestly state. But perhaps the most telling problem with the priesthood today is the loss of perception of its own identity. Just what is a priest supposed to do today? What makes him different from a good Catholic layman? If the only things that are proper to his state of life are the presidency at the Eucharist and the absolving of sins, are these really enough to justify such a different life-style? Does there have to be a priestly caste, living a life apart from and diverse from the laity, just to do these things? Why does the sacrament of orders demand a radical change in a person's manner of living, whereas the other sacraments of priesthood, baptism and confirmation, require only a Christian way of life? Why could not the life of the priest be indistinguishable from that of the good Christian layman with the single exception that the priest would be empowered to administer the sacraments, and, given the occasion, would so do?

Questions like these were bound to arise in the post-Vatican II Church. Vatican II looks much more benignly upon the world and its standards than did the Council of Trent. It admits the greater competency of the laity in certain areas even of religious endeavor. Enlistment of lay people in the works of Catholic Action for decades prior to the Council proved to the hierarchy not only their capability of functioning in areas not open to the clergy, but also their superiority in some domains which seemed in the past to have been the private preserve of priests. It is, of course, in the liturgy and in the parish CCD programs that the resultant action of the Council has become most apparent to Catholics at large and has undoubtedly raised in their mind a question about the proper task of the priest. Not a few of the laity, hearing their neighbor reading the epistle at Mass, or learning from their children how a catechism class was conducted by the lady who lives two blocks away, or seeing their own relative distribute Communion, have been tempted to sing to their priests: "Anything you can do, we can do better!"

But the secularizing trends of Vatican II have had an even greater impact on priests themselves. It all began rather quietly with the issue of retirement. Before the Council it was unthinkable that a priest who was still willing and able to work spend his declining years in any role but that of pastor of a flock. But today the standards of secular life are applied. To be sure, one remains a priest forever, but his active ministry may be terminated by his superior when he reaches a compulsory retirement age. The chain of reasoning set off by this consideration led to advocacy of part-time ministerial service by some. So-called hyphenated priests began to appear: priest-psychologists, priest-sociologists, priest-counselors, priest-lawyers; priest-entrepreneurs of all sorts. With the greater participation of the laity in administrative parochial tasks, in liturgy teams, in financial boards, in parish councils, the idea of participatory parochial management by teams of priests rather than by a canonical pastor was advanced. Priests' senates and associations proliferated and at times began to wield unprecedented power over diocesan affairs. Of course the Council envisioned the senate as only an advisory body to the bishop. But once the camel's nose was under the tent the possibilities for power plays of one kind or another loomed large. The structure even of religious orders began to be modified along more democratic lines until finally the customary Vatican guidelines appeared. Right now the phenomenon of a permanent diaconate encompassing married men who will continue in many dioceses to hold secular jobs while engaging in a part-time or weekend ministry is creating a flurry of speculation in ecclesiastical circles. What will be the relationship of these men, empowered to do almost everything but say Mass and hear confessions, to their pastor and his associates and to the bishop himself? What will a promise of obedience mean in the case of a man who does not depend for his livelihood upon the hierarchy? Does embracing the clerical state for a person who will live with his wife and family and pursue his secular career have any meaning at all? Will the deacons have a distinctive dress, a different life-style from their lay confreres? Will they eventually replace priests and emerge as the chief order of ministers? Will they have their own labor union and negotiate with the bishop through it? Will they demonstrate once and for all that neither celibacy nor a full-blown theological education is needed for effective ministry? Will they so identify with their lay charges as to widen further the rift between priest and people? Where will it all end?

If today's priests experience a certain schizophrenia it is quite understandable. The theology and priestly culture of the recent past made them understand that they were men set apart for the service of the Lord. But the practicalities of their working lives today make them understand that if they are to succeed they must be identified with their people, and not despise, but assume and live in accordance with their values. Yet the Gospel excoriates both the Pharisees who considered themselves men set apart by their religious traditions, and the Zealots who equated Israel's religious activities with its political ambitions and secular goals. The working through of a synthesis between the eschatological and purely religious aspects of priestly life on the one hand, and the incarnational and secular ones on the other, remains as much a problem in today's sophisticated society as it was in New Testament times. Following the lead of past eras which have alternately experienced the stronger attraction of one polarity or the other, today's priesthood, in lieu of a workable synthesis, will have to adjust and allow itself to be drawn principally by that view which will best serve the human needs of the modern world.

To be sure, the Roman Catholic Church places great emphasis upon tradition. This is hardly one of its weaknesses,

but rather an immense source of strength. Today's problems
will never be exactly the same as past ones. Not even the
most conservative person would claim that, for the world does
progress or regress, and issues change. But the traditionalist
position would assert, and rightly so, that the past can and
has to illumine the decisions of the present; that the course
set in the present cannot deviate substantially from the original one set long ago in the past, and that the present has no
right to pass judgment upon the past except in relation to its
own standards, not according to current ones. The real difficulty that the Church has experienced in coming to grips today with the yin and yang of religiosity and secularity in the
lives of its diocesan priests has not sprung from its adherence
to tradition. Rather it has originated from a lack of awareness
of that tradition prior to the Council of Trent. Indeed the
scholar in the Church has not been ignorant of the history of
the diocesan priesthood from very early times. But until recently there has been little communication between scholars
and those who have the decision-making power in the community. Consequently official action has been taken largely with
only the norms set down by the Council of Trent and subsequent legislation inspired by them as the traditional foundation and backdrop. Yet the Council of Trent for reasons that
shall appear in the course of the development of this chapter
was highly partisan to the solution of the problem of priestly
life-style by adherence to an almost totally religious pattern.
But it was not always thus.

The history of the diocesan clergy from days removed only
by a generation or so from St. Paul, who worked at the trade
he had learned as a rabbi even while he was involved with the
preaching of the word, down to the days of the Cardinals
Richelieu and Mazarin, who were chief ministers of state for
the French kings, indicates a deep and intimate involvement
with purely secular affairs. First, it will be helpful to adduce
some data indicative of the fact that before the Council of

Trent at least some segments of the clergy did embrace in addition to their priestly duties positions in government or military service, or jobs as artisans or farmers, Secondly, it would be proper to consider the legality of such activities in the light of the decrees of the various councils and synods.

As might be suspected, there is not a wealth of historical material dealing with the life-style of the diocesan priest in the pre-Tridentine era. But there is considerable information about their leaders, the bishops. Of course, it has been proposed from relatively early times in the Church that the primary responsibility for the preaching of the Gospel and the setting of an example for both lower clergy and the laity rests primarily with the bishops. If we, therefore, find the leaders of the Christian community immersed in secular affairs, it would not seem totally illogical to conclude that their clergy, in quite a different social context, of course, were similarly involved.

The life-style of bishops in the early Church was hardly significantly different from that of their counterparts in the secular nobility. Most bishops came from noble families. It seems true that in very early times they were elected by the people. One has only to think of the case of St. Ambrose. This initial apparently spontaneous popular movement, however, did not in the course of time burgeon into a democratic process, even in those places where there is evidence that it might have lasted for some years. With very few exceptions, as the Church grew, episcopal dynasties developed. Originally the people undoubtedly chose some outstanding ancient member of these sacerdotal clans as their spiritual leader. But in the course of time they were content with letting the issue become a family affair governed only by the laws of inheritance and the decisions of the head of the house. In other words, like the political hegemony, the spiritual leadership became dynastic, and the same family which provided its first son as prince or governor very likely offered its second son as bishop of the region. Later on heads of states claimed the right to elect bishops on the grounds that they were the legitimate representatives of the people, who originally enjoyed that right, before the family tradition was established. As late as 1957 President René Coty of France appointed A. Elchinger coadjutor bishop of Strasbourg in virtue of this claim. With the publication in 1972 of new norms for the nomination of bishops the Holy See has asked heads of state to give up any privileges they still claim in this regard. Similarly, in virtue of the selfsame argument, in the eleventh century Council of the Lateran which reserved the right to elect a pope to the cardinals, some veto power was recognized on the part of the Roman Emperor. Later on in the seventeenth century veto rights in papal elections were claimed by several kings. It is said that in the conclave of 1655 Cardinal Sacchetti was actually elected pope, but was excluded by a Spanish veto with the result that Fabio Chigi became Alexander VII. Early in the twentieth century Pope Pius X repudiated all powers of veto in papal elections claimed by various secular authorities.

Polycrates of Ephesus is one of our chief witnesses regarding the dynastic system. Challenged relative to his keeping of the traditions of the Church, he proposes to Pope St. Victor a clinching argument for his authority as bishop: "I observe the traditions of those of my family in whose footsteps I follow; seven of my forebears were bishops, and I am the eighth."

St. Gregory of Nazianz began his ecclesiastical career as an apprentice to his father, and later succeeded him as bishop. Two of his cousins were also bishops. A chronicler of Limoges in France notes something which seems to be exceptional: Ruricius the bishop of that see was succeeded in office not by his son, but by his grandson.

Some of the best-known bishop-saints of this early period of the Church's development were married men and part and parcel of the dynastic system. Among them we can number

Germain of Auxerre, Hilary of Poitiers and Synesius of Cyrene as outstanding both in doctrine and holiness of life.

Because such a dynastic system, fostering control, as it did, of both ecclesiastical and political affairs by the same family, led to a number of abuses, it was opposed by certain bourgeois critics of the nobility. Large estates and properties handed down by the laws of heredity became the concern of the hierarchy. Priests were often assigned the management of these holdings. St. John Chrysostom mentions some who were so occupied in supervising castles and estates, in caring for the harvests and wine making, and in promoting the sale of fruit and grain in the market place that they found little time for their religious duties. Such abuses enraged writers like St. Jerome. In his correspondence with Eustochium he rants and raves about clerical playboys and swingers who spent large amounts of time entertaining or being entertained by rich dowagers. The fiery scholar laid the cause of such excesses at the door of the system itself, which seemed to neglect Gospel values. No doubt it was his bitter opposition to this dynastic control of the Church that prompted him to unfold his rather refreshing and astounding theory about the origins of the episcopacy through the action of a few power-grabbing priests.

We may be tempted to forget that seminaries originated only in the sixteenth century. Some of the bishops in the early Church were great theologians, but many of them knew no theology at all. Sometimes a man like St. Ambrose was chosen bishop because of his great learning; but Ambrose's proficiency as a scholar lay in the area of letters and philosophy, not that of theology. Bishop Synesius of Cyrene was a renowned poet and philosopher. At the time of his episcopal ordination he knew no theology at all. In fact, at the time of his election to the bishopric of Cyrene he, like Ambrose, was not even a Christian as yet! It is likewise interesting to note that the greatest apologists for Christianity in the earliest centuries, men like Justin, Minucius Felix, Tertullian, Arnobius and

Origen (who later was forced to become a priest to maintain his teaching post), were not bishops at all, but laymen.

If bishops in general during this very early period of ecclesiastical history were not adept in theology, neither were priests. In fact, in certain areas in the West it was not only by custom, but also by law that priests were prohibited from preaching the word. The right to preach was, of course, the bishop's in the first instance. But many bishops, sensing their own inadequacy in technical matters, would empower and authorize laymen trained in theology to preach to as well as to teach large assemblies of catechumens and faithful. Best known indeed is the case of Origen, who conducted the famous school of theology at Alexandria. Though he was not allowed to preach by his own ordinary on the grounds that he was only a layman, he was granted full faculties to preach and teach by the bishops of Jerusalem and Caesarea. Later when he returned to his own diocese he allowed himself to be ordained so he could preach.

Later on in the history of the Church priests were given an apprentice or in-service type training by their bishop or a priest selected by him. Those who were sent by their bishop to the monastic schools received a more academic orientation and were introduced to the study of theology and law. With the rise of the great European universities in the thirteenth century theological education improved, and those candidates for the priesthood who were fortunate enough to be sent by their ordinaries to these centers of learning received a hitherto unprecedented theological training.

Because of their connection with powerful noble families, in the early period of the history of the Church bishops were often called upon to assume positions of responsibility in the royal or imperial court. Bedollière attests that during the fourth and fifth centuries in France large numbers of bishops became senators, governors of provinces, proprietors of large estates and imperial officers. Guizot states that in the fifth century bishops and priests became the principal municipal magistrates also. Much earlier St. Cyprian had inveighed against pastors who deserted their flocks to take over the management of property or assume control of business establishments for the sake of filthy lucre. He might have been thinking of men like Dorotheus, a priest of Antioch, who was appointed by the Emperor a customs official to take charge of all cloth imports from Tyre. Some modern commentators opine that modern ecclesiastical titles like "monsignor, my Lord, your Excellency, your Grace, your Eminence, your Serenity, your Amplitude," etc. came into usage not because of the position the title bearer held in the Church, where in accordance with the Gospel injunction office was to be viewed as a service of humility, but because of his governmental rank. The alliance of Church and state achieved during this period in the person of so many bishops was undoubtedly one of the factors that led eventually to the investiture controversy of later times when secular authorities claimed some rights in the choice and installation of bishops.

When in the tenth century in the flourishing feudal system bishops had become temporal barons in their own right, they also, like their lay counterparts, assumed the role of ministers of justice in their own right. Seemingly, however, out of respect for their clerical status most of them disqualified themselves from meting out or executing a sentence of death. Their knowledge of law was one of their chief assets in this role, and they encouraged those who would succeed them to become familiar with the rapidly growing collections of decretals and edicts of both civil and canonical origin. Tours of duty at the imperial or royal court familiarized many of them with administrative proceedings in many areas and on a rather large scale, and so enhanced their own prowess when they returned to their own domain.

In later times, of course, many high ecclesiastics devoted their whole life to service at court. Most familiar are the names of Richelieu and Mazarin, but the Cardinals d'Estrees, Forbin-Janson, Fleury, Dubois, Tencin, Bernis and Retz served in a similar vein. Richelieu himself employed Cardinal Bérulle as his foreign minister, Cardinal de la Valette as commander of his armies and Archbishop Sourdis as admiral of his fleet. At the court of Louis XIV there were five different grades of almoners or public aid officials, all staffed by ecclesiastics. A veritable horde of clerics occupied other positions at court, from that of prime minister down to that of royal musician, whose duty it was to provide accompaniment for dances and ballets and state dinners.

History also records a few cases involving high ecclesiastical dignitaries in significant but definitely more menial civil occupations. Urban renewal has for a longer time than many suspect been considered to be one of the important services that a government supplies for its citizenry. The historian Sicard commemorates a certain Monseigneur de Barrol, bishop of Castres, who was celebrated as a carpenter, geometrician and architect. It was he who rearranged, laid out and worked on the streets and boulevards of his see-city.

Of course, even in these later periods there were some who took up the cudgel once wielded by St. Jerome. The secular involvement of so many of the clergy and its implication for the layman were not passed over without notice. In 1781, for instance, a publication entitled *Secret Letters on the Actual State of Religion and of the Clergy* acrimoniously attacked bishops and priests who deserted their dioceses to rob the laity of jobs more suited to them.

The Italian writer Vespasiano adds to the list of higher ecclesiastics whom we know to have been involved full-time in governmental positions during the era of the Renaissance. Piero da Monte, the bishop of Brescia, was also civil governor of Perugia. Francesco Bertini, bishop of Capaccio, was ambassador to the King of England. Niccolò Perotto, the bishop of Sipontino, held several state offices. The archbishop of

Strigonia ruled Bohemia in the name of King Mathias. The bishop of Cologne became chancellor of a king, and employed a priest as his personal librarian and archivist.

Many bishops and priests in these early centuries, if they could not find employment in the ministries of state, launched upon a military career. The *Song of Roland* commemorates Archbishop Turpin, who led his troops against the Turks; he was one of the most popular heroes among the medieval clergy. Spencer states that in the seventh century in France bishops regularly went into battle with their lay counterparts, and by the middle of the eighth century military service on the part of the clergy was an accepted fact. Under Charles Martel it was common to see bishops and priests bearing arms. Guizot indicates that bishops not only took part in the national warfare, which might have served the common good, but at times, due to the fact that they had under their command efficient mercenaries, undertook expeditions of rapine and violence against their neighbors on their own account. Orderic describes several musterings of lay troops under the captaincy of the clergy in France: one in 1094, and again in 1108 and 1119. Even after the middle of the fifteenth century Cardinal de Balue assembled his troops in Paris and made a display of military might. It was not until after the middle of the seventeenth century in France that a government edict exempted the clergy from personal military service.

In England when King Richard the Lion-Hearted was asked by the papal legate to that country to free Philippe de Dreux, the bishop of Beauvais, whom he held prisoner, because Philippe was an ecclesiastic and his rights to immunity ought to have been observed, Richard indignantly replied that Philippe had not been captured as a bishop, but as a knight in full armor, a knight moreover who was a "robber, tyrant and incendiary," one who spent day and night in devastating Richard's lands. At the famous battle of Agincourt the bishop of Sens was killed, not ministering as a chaplain to his country's troops, but, sword in hand like a true soldier, shouting bloody murder against the English.

There is evidence also that in Rome itself as late as the fourteenth century popes and cardinals employed clerics who were not fortunate enough to obtain curial posts in their private armies and bodyguards. Cardinal Pedro de Luna, for instance, maintained a garrison in which a number of clerics held key positions. One of these specially commended was a certain Arnaldus Vich, priest and bombardier.

Though we do not have as much direct evidence for the involvement of priests in secular activities as we do in the case of bishops, simply because history tends to take more note of leaders or persons of prominence, as was said before, we can presume that priests took the lead from their bishops. This presumption becomes all the more valid when we consider the condition of the lower clergy in ancient times. Priests generally did not come from the nobility. They were not rich in their own right. Nor could they be sustained from the meager collections of foodstuffs offered by the laity in the course of the liturgy each Sunday. (Up until the fourth or fifth century daily Mass was not a common thing at all; indeed, even the Sunday liturgies seem to have been populated by only the most devout.) So it became absolutely necessary for them to become artisans or take up some trade if they were able to, or to till the fields. This conclusion, as we shall see, is supported by early legislation in the Church.

Fleury adduces a case in point when he writes that the bishop-saint John the Almoner ordained to the priesthood one of his lectors, a holy shoemaker, who had a great number of children. This man continued to work at his trade, but was nonetheless assiduous in promoting the welfare of the Church. Fleury also states that at Alexandria in the early Church there were great numbers of married priests who were artisans or tradesmen.

Another argument can be adduced from the fact that in later times it was essential to the economic welfare of certain countries which had an extremely large population of priests that they engage in trade or agriculture. In Spain during the reign of Philip II when a more or less accurate census was taken, it revealed that nearly one quarter of the adult population was listed in the ranks of the secular or regular clergy. There were approximately 312,000 diocesan priests and 400,-000 religious. Two centuries earlier in France an ecclesiastical visitation discloses an average of ten priests per parish in the sparsely populated, poor rural area not far from Nantes. Around the same time the small diocese of Constance ordained an average of two hundred priests per year. At the time of the Hussite revolt one third of the total assets of the Bohemian nation was in the hands of the clergy.

Despite the notion inculcated by Vatican II that bishops must be concerned not only about their own proper dioceses but also share some responsibility for the operation of the Church at large, priests today are bound by incardination to remain in the diocese to which they were attached by admission into the clerical state. It is not easy for them to be released for service elsewhere even though the talents that appear after a number of years of ministry might be better utilized in a new locale. Then too, priests are not free to leave the parish to which they have been assigned by their bishop without his permission or letter of reassignment. But it was not always thus in the Church. In the late Middle Ages there were not only great numbers of itinerant seculars, but even considerable numbers of regulars, monks and friars, wandering from place to place throughout Europe. Often papal decrees had to be issued not only in relation to them, warning them to return to their home dioceses and religious houses, but also against vagrant bishops, hangers-on at the papal, royal and princely courts. Wandering bishops became a problem in Ireland in the twelfth century. With regard to parish assignments in feudal times, in many places a system was employed which has some similarities with that in vogue in some Protestant circles today. It was the responsibility of the liege lord of a particular locale to provide religious services for the villagers, the serfs, who labored on his estates. Prospective pastors negotiated with the lord of the manor and his council, and when terms agreeable to both sides were reached, the priest was hired for this service. He was then empowered by the bishop of the area to perform all of the sacred rites for his charges in accordance with the canon law of the time. Even as late as the seventeenth century in Switzerland there is evidence of a custom in some areas not only of an initial contract of service drawn up between parishioners and their pastor, but of a yearly ceremony of renewal, during which the agreement could be rescinded by either party.

The cases we have considered are but a few examples of the secular involvement of the diocesan clergy in the pre-Tridentine Church. The fact that there were often gross abuses arising from this system cannot be denied. In fact, the scandalous situations are so well known that they need not be dwelt upon. The post-Tridentine era has not known a pope like Alexander VI or John XII. Nor has any synod echoed the complaint of that held in Trosly in 909: "The whole world is replete with lechery and adultery; church-money is appropriated, and the poor are murdered and neglected." It is the legislation emanating from pre-Tridentine times that is our chief source of knowledge about the life of the lower clergy of that period. As time passes regulations prohibiting certain kinds of secular involvement become more and more stringent. Undoubtedly most of these rules were issued to correct abuses; they are not always evidence of an anti-worldly attitude in the minds of those who had chief responsibility for the carrying out of the Church's apostolic mission. Just how did legislation in the pre-Tridentine Church sanction and limit the secular spirit and life-style of the clergy? Was the *de facto* secular involvement, samples of which we have just presented, a condition which prevailed in spite of or in accord with the spirit of the ecclesiastical laws of the period? These are the questions which we must now consider.

At first glance it would seem that clerical engagement in secular business was forbidden by long-standing legislation. The third canon of the Council of Chalcedon (451) states very clearly: "No bishop, cleric or monk shall engage in secular traffic or business, except in the interest of minors, orphans or other needy persons." Really the key to the interpretation of this decree is the exception that it notes. Many clerics, as we have seen, had become involved in business dealings of various kinds for reasons of self-aggrandizement. Against such St. Jerome, St. John Chrysostom and others had inveighed most vehemently. Selfishness was always considered a motive unbecoming one who assumed the role of an *alter Christus,* one who dedicated himself to the service of others as Christ had done. In the preamble to this legislation the Council itself explains the reason for the prohibition: "It has come to the knowledge of the holy Council that some members of the clergy for sordid gain have become tenants of the estates of others and engage in secular occupations, neglecting the service of God, insinuating themselves into the houses of people of the world, and from covetous motives undertake the administration of their property." It is not that secular work as such is condemned; what is reprehensible is that such jobs should be undertaken for reasons of personal gain to the neglect of ecclesiastical duties and detriment to the welfare of the Church.

This decree is most important, because it set a precedent for all subsequent ecclesiastical legislation relating to the secular involvement of clerics. The interpretation given was reflected in other councils and synods down through the centuries. Provided that it did not lead to the neglect of ecclesiastical responsibilities, and that it was not undertaken out of greedy personal motives but rather to help the indigent (including the cleric himself, if he was truly poor), secular work was not to be regarded as an evil, but rather as a benefit to clerical life.

Hincmar of Rheims reports that the Council of Nantes decreed the following program as ideal for the carrying out of a truly priestly life. Every day priests should first recite the canonical hours for the benefit of their people. Then they should visit the sick of their parish and administer the sacraments to those seeking them. Finally, if they have the ability to do so, they should go out to labor in the fields that they might be able to succour pilgrims, the sick and the bereaved.

In Africa in 429 the Fourth Council of Carthage declared that it was good for priests, provided that it could be done without prejudicing their ecclesiastical duties, to provide themselves with food and clothing by engaging in farming or plying some trade so as not to become a burden to the laity. Canon 51 of this Council states very clearly: "A cleric, howsoever learned he might be in the word of God, must support himself by learning some trade."

Through a kind of osmosis this legislation aimed at the diocesan clergy had also an influence on monastic life. St. Benedict viewed work in the fields or at some trade as an essential part of the spiritual life of his charges. Manual labor was prescribed by his rule. Sometimes in fulfillment of this injunction work was undertaken even outside the monastery properties. The Carolingian Capitularies indicate that the secular authorities took advantage of this provision of the rule of St. Benedict to persuade the abbots of certain monasteries to employ their charges in both road building and repair in the kingdom, as well as to use them in the work of ministering to the poor and destitute. Later on Abelard lamented the neglect of manual labor in many monasteries of his time. "We who ought," he wrote, "to live by the labor of our own hands (which alone, as St. Benedict said, truly makes us monks) now cultivate idleness, the subtle enemy of our soul, and seek

our livelihood from the labors of other men." Abbot Peter the
Venerable sought to correct this abuse: "We have ordained,"
he averred, "that the ancient and holy custom of manual labor
should be restored. . . ."

If the monasteries patterned their life-style upon that of the
secular clergy, largely preoccupied as they were in the days of
St. Benedict with tilling the fields or plying some trade, there
is no reason to doubt that some of the later military religious
orders patterned themselves after the model of the priest-sol-
dier of their time.

This osmosis of life-style from the secular clergy into religious orders was indeed a curious phenomenon of history,
for it was understood from the beginning that the religious
was a person who for the sake of devoting himself entirely to
God and to prayer had to flee from the world. Equally as
curious in later times, as we shall see, was the counterflow of
the osmotic current from the religious house into the rectory.

At the time of the decree of Gratian we find a basic recapit-
ulation of the same principle announced in earlier legislation:
"Clerics who for the sake of filthy lucre or by means of dishon-
est transactions provide for themselves must learn how to live
off of the offerings of the faithful. But if what comes through
the Church is not adequate to support a cleric decently, let
him provide for his needs by engaging in a trade or farming
after the example of the Apostle (who lived by the work of
his hands) but in such a way that he does not neglect the
vigils of the Church. . . ." The decretals indicate that a priest
is sufficiently prepared for his ministry to the Church if he
knows how to read or render by heart the book of the sacraments, the lectionaries, antiphonals, the order of baptism,
the penitential canon, and the psalter; and if he is able to give
appropriate homilies on Sundays and the greater feasts of the
Church. In addition he must know how to add and to provide
for himself by learning a trade or farming.

The theoretical issue of secularizing and anti-secular strains in the New Testament and very early Christian literature came to a head with the establishment of the mendicant orders in the thirteenth century. The mendicants were religious who borrowed their ethos partly from the diocesan clergy and partly from the monastic institutions. Like the seculars they sought their own sanctification in ministry to the people, not in separation from the world. Like the monks, they vowed a life of poverty, but interpreted it to mean that the order itself, as well as the individual friars comprising it, would not be permitted to hold property of any kind.

The anti-worldly spirit of the Gospels is brought to bear upon the life of the overseers of the Christian community in the pastoral epistles. The ideal set before Timothy and Titus seems at times quite clerical. The former is urged to labor like a soldier of Jesus Christ; he is warned not to implicate himself in the "business-affairs of life" (2 Tim 2:4). Yet in Acts, First Corinthians and First and Second Thessalonians we find clear references to the fact that Paul himself practiced the trade that he had learned in accordance with rabbinical law even while he served as an apostle of Jesus Christ. His motive was not to become a burden to the communities he served. The apocryphal *Acts of Thomas* depicts that Apostle as a carpenter who exercised his craft while on mission in India. In fact, the *Acts* reports that he was commissioned by King Gunafor to build a palace for him. Eusebius points out that the grandsons of the Apostle Jude not only because of their connection as "relatives of the Lord" but also because of their witnessing of the faith before the Emperor Domitian became "leaders of the churches." He borrows from Hegesippus the information that they were farmers, working their land to raise money to pay taxes and otherwise support themselves by their honest toil.

This yin and yang of early opinion might have been brought about by the persuasion rife among some believers that since the Parousia was imminent an all-out effort ought to be made to disseminate the message of the Gospel. There simply could be no time for secular affairs. But when in the course of time this expectation was not realized, the excitement passed, and the practical exigencies of life reasserted themselves. At any rate more serious polarization was effected when William of St. Amour, secular priest and theologian at the University of Paris, bitterly attacked the Franciscans shortly after their establishment in the thirteenth century. He argued that all tradition shows that any Christian, be he cleric or layman, should not seek to live off the labors of others if he is able to work himself. He points out that the Apostle Paul commanded that if an able person refuses to work, he should not eat. Moreover, the Apostle set an example himself, when in the midst of his very trying and enervating missionary labors and travels, he supported himself by returning for some periods of time to the craft of tentmaking. William concludes his argument: "It is not therefore an unlawful thing, but very much in accord with good morality for not only nobles and men of learning, but for priests and preachers as well, for those who have left everything for the sake of Christ, to engage in manual labor for their sustenance: to become farmers, artisans, builders, tailors, or to hold any kind of an honorable job. . . ." Indeed, the enthusiastic supporters of William in their frenzy against the mendicants seemed to imply that, in the case of the able-bodied, manual labor was necessary for salvation.

Severinus Binius, a sixteenth-century commentator on ecclesiastical decrees, presents a veritable bonanza of information when he considers the edicts of the Fourth Council of Carthage. We learn from St. Augustine, he states, that at the time of the Council the Massiliani (semi-Pelagian heretics from Marseilles in France) had followers in Africa who were teaching that it was not licit for the clergy to engage in manual labor. In accordance with the teaching of the Gospel, God's ministers above all his people were to trust in his providence, and believe that God would care for them and sustain them from the free-will offerings of others. Binius states that this doctrine of the Massiliani contradicts both the teaching and example of St. Paul. So the Fourth Council of Carthage was at pains to repudiate it. He bolsters his argument against Massilianism with several other proofs. He adduces the Constitution of Pope Clement in which, he says, young clerics are warned not to become wards of the Church, but to follow the example of the apostles, who were very loath to put any extra burden on the laity. So, setting aside from time to time the task of preaching the word, they devoted themselves to manual labor, some as fishermen, others as tentmakers and still others as farmers. Justin Martyr, too, touches the case in point when he commends labor as a God-given means of supplying one's legitimate human needs and of alleviating the misery of the poor. Epiphanius tells of priests of his time who, while continuing to preach the word, imitated "their holy father in Christ, Paul, providing thus not only for themselves, but also for their indigent brothers"; such labor merits the highest praise, and sets a good example for others. Thus according to Binius the whole tradition of the Church has borne testimony to the correctness of the decision of the Council.

Another writer close to the time of the Council of Trent, St. Robert Bellarmine, addressing himself to this question, tries to steer a course between the Scylla of Massilianism, which teaches that secular work is forbidden to the clergy, and the Charybdis of Anti-mendicancy, which holds that manual labor is absolutely necessary for salvation. He intimates that for the religious and secular clergy alike, manual labor might be necessary, not indeed for salvation, but to provide a reasonably decent sustenance, to offset idleness and ward off temptation.

The legal principle set down in the Council of Chalcedon that secular labor is commendable for clerics provided that it does not interfere with ecclesiastical responsibilities and is not undertaken out of greed or selfishness was substantially main-

tained down to the time of the Council of Trent. Local decrees, however, sought to specify what kind of occupations
could not be tolerated either because they necessarily implied
curtailment of clerical duties or were outrageously lucrative,
or a source of scandal to the laity, or simply against good ecclesiastical discipline. Typical are the Council at Carthage in
398 which warns priests not to become pimps or to engage in
disreputable work of any kind, and another in the same city
in 436 which suspended from office priests indulging themselves in scurrilous activities or jocular repartee, and threatened with excommunication those entertaining dinner guests
with song, the Council of Trullo (692) forbidding priests to
take jobs as actors; that of Friuli (796) interdicting the play-
ing of musical instruments in secular orchestras. An attempt
was made by the Council of Tribur (895) to prevent priests
from accepting governmental positions of honor or jobs in the
military. Even the secular authority was concerned about some
clerical jobs. The decrees of King Edgar discourage clerics
from becoming brewers or barmen. The Synod of Valentia
(1261) tried to outlaw the carrying of arms by the clergy,
while the Council of Tarragona (1317) warned them against
accepting jobs on pirate ships or engaging in any acts of piracy
except those against infidels. Most inclusive in its list of interdicted jobs for the clergy is the Synod of Liège (1287), which
forbade them to become money-changers, executioners, tavern
keepers, fullers, tailors, garment fitters, actors, comedians,
woodsmen, millers, perfumers, courtiers, bailiffs, tax collectors
and tripe mongers.

The Council of Trent established a trend away from the
secular that had a lasting and remarkable effect upon the
priesthood in recent times. There can be no doubt that
throughout Renaissance days abuses had become so rampant
and so scandalous that drastic and effective reform was absolutely necessary. It is to the everlasting credit of the Council
that it was able to achieve that reform. But there were three

basic causal factors at play that enabled the pendulum to
swing from one extreme to another, from a position of over-
extended secular involvement to one of almost monastic flight
and isolation.

At the root of the phenomenon is the ambivalence of the issue in the New Testament itself. In this area, as in so many
others, on the practical decisional level, a double message
seems to be given. Thanks to the Massiliani and William of
St. Amour we have an impressive collection of texts on both
sides. The truly dedicated believer is to trust in the providence
of God; yet St. Paul knew how to take care of himself by
working with his hands. Christ is described in the Epistle to
the Hebrews as a priest who is fully otherworldly, one separated from the things of this world; yet the Gospels depict
him as being so involved with secular affairs and with sinners
that he shocked those who claimed to be the separated ones,
the Pharisees. The world is described at one time as a field
ripe with grain to be harvested, and at another as the enemy
of the soul. And so it goes throughout almost every significant
section of the New Testament. Ultimately one is left to make
his own decision as to how he is to survive in this life and still
be intent upon the next, as to how he is to be totally concerned about his soul without neglecting the basic needs of his
body. And for whatever position he takes he will be able to
find justification from the texts of Scripture itself. With rare
insight Pope Alexander IV in his Bull *Romanus Pontifex*
condemning the ideas of William of St. Amour hit upon the
central problem of not only the case in point but of Christianity itself as a traditional religion when he wrote: "Some people, believing that they understand Sacred Scripture, but
straying from the path of right reason, have hatched out new
evils in the Church . . . and risen to speak falsely against
their brothers. . . ." Was it not in defense of the Gospel
message, a defense that itself falsified the most fundamental
principle of that message, that the Inquisition was established,

that during Reformation times bloody persecution raged, and closer to our own era a spirit of animosity and suspicion against other Christians was fostered?

A second reason is to be found in the seeming simplicity but actual complexity of the norm that was set down originally in the Council of Chalcedon and guided the Church until the Renaissance. That norm, as we have said, permitted secular involvement under two conditions: first, secularity was not to impede or interfere with the ecclesiastical responsibilities that ordination brought; and secondly, it was not to be embraced out of personal greed or ambition, but only to alleviate one's own necessities and to provide for the poor and destitute. Now not even today with all of our sophistication have we been able clearly to draw the line between necessity and superfluity. It all depends, we say, on the situation; the guidelines have to be relative. Some bishops because of their position, because of what is expected of them, may actually need a mansion and large estates; some priests may actually need a Cadillac. Surveys reveal that a number of priests today have abandoned the recitation of the Divine Office. Some undoubtedly have done so to make more time to devote to people and their problems. Once again even in our time the line of demarcation between what are the ecclesiastical responsibilities assumed upon ordination and what are not cannot be clearly and definitely established. Perhaps too, history has shown the norm to be unworkable because it is too idealistic. It presumes too much. It presupposes that priests will always be able to be unselfish and devoted to their responsibilities to the Church. But from the clear teaching of St. Paul the leaders of the Church should have realized that whatever purity of life a Christian has is the result of the operation of God's grace in him. And that grace is not to be presumed. It must remain always the perfectly free gift of divine benevolence, even in a Church that has some assurance of receiving it.

The third reason is surely the most significant one. Between the secular and religious priesthood there was always in evidence a close bond of brotherhood. Though theoretically their life-styles were notably different, in practice an osmotic influence between the parish church and the monastic chapel has always been in evidence. As was indicated, St. Benedict very likely got his idea for a rule demanding manual labor from the practice of the diocesan clergy of his time, and orders like the Knights Templars who served so well during the Crusades may well have been influenced by the military escapades of certain bishop-knights and their clergy. But the vital flow moved in the opposite direction also. And there can be little doubt that the mendicant orders which arose in the thirteenth century presented an ethos which was very radical for religious. It really removed them from the monastery and placed them side by side with the diocesan clergy in the apostolate. Up until this time the very essence of religious life centered upon personal perfection. The religious traditionally was identified as one who worked primarily for his own spiritual advancement, and only in an indirect way (presumably), through prayer and sacrifice, for the salvation to others. The work of the secular priest, on the other hand, pivoted around concern for others; he worked directly for the salvation of his people and through that work hoped also to perfect himself spiritually. Except for the fact that they exempted themselves from the authority of those who on the local scene were traditionally responsible for the apostolate, the bishops, and placed themselves through their superiors directly under the apostolic mission of the pope himself, the mendicant orders in their work objectives, though not in their personal life-style, were indistinguishable from the seculars. They too strove for the salvation of others in accordance with their institutes, for example, by modeling for the world evangelical poverty and its value, not behind monastery walls, but in the market place (Franciscans) or by the ministry of preaching (Dominicans). So they were unlike any religious hitherto known, and seemed to be taking over the job of the bishops and secular priests while repudiating their life-style. That is why the animus of conservative theologians like William of St. Amour was aroused against them. But the strangest thing of all was that they, though fully committed to the apostolate, took the vows of evangelical perfection which traditionally implied sequestration from the world and primary dedication to personal sanctification. Here then was the bizarre anomaly that was destined eventually to reverse completely the osmotic process. These orders essayed the seemingly impossible; they tried to unite opposites: the flight from the world implied in the vows which demanded giving up the things that the world valued most, riches, marriage and personal independence on the one hand; and the mission to the world in the midst of the world demanded by apostolic activity on the other. And the miracle is that they succeeded! In general they won the respect and admiration of the laity. So when the diocesan clergy stood in need of reform, and the Council of Trent had neither the means nor the time to search out alternative solutions to its problem, the transfer of the life-style of the mendicants to the secular clergy became a relatively simple matter.

Today while planning what the priest must be in the future we certainly must ponder what he was in the past. It may be no more than a truism to state that one who is prepared to ignore the past may be doomed to repeat it. But it is unconscionable in an institution dedicated to the preservation of tradition to be uninformed about that tradition. There can really be no return to the past. That is most fortunate, because no one would want to return to the past. But there is a future for the priesthood. And it is the priests of the present who must shape that future. And they must undertake that task with not merely the memory of the recent past, against which perhaps many would tend to react, but with a far-reaching backward glance, one that will take them to eras when priestly existence was quite different, when factors were at play that may again loom large in the future. In that backward glance they must surely let their eyes rest for a moment on the pregnant words of Pope Celestine I, who in the fifth century wrote to the priests of France: "It is not by what we wear that we priests are different from the laity; it is rather by our teaching and profession of the faith—not by the type of uniform we wear, but by our exemplary conduct—in fact, it is not by anything external at all, but by the purity of our spirit."

CHAPTER II
The Priestly Charism

Life-style is only one element to be considered in contemplating the priesthood in our time and in the future. While, as we have tried to show, it has varied considerably throughout the ages, it has not affected a reality postulated by all theologies and theories of the priesthood, the unchangeable essence of priestliness. This essence, presumably, has come down from the very earliest times of the Church's existence, remains with us today and will have to be preserved, no matter what else goes, in the time to come. It is, however, a most elusive thing, that priestly essence. Down through the ages theologians and researchers have tried to put their finger on it with the result that numerous theoretical views and perspectives have been advanced. It will be the purpose of this chapter to search out that essential element in priestly existence with the help of past as well as more recent speculation.

It was the contention of the German philosopher Friedrich Nietzsche that the highest values in human life tend eventually to devaluate themselves. Or rather society brings about their depreciation. The highest values that man knows are personal ones. They are the charismatic gifts of individuals who make an impact upon and better the condition of man-

kind. But time is the enemy of these values. Life must necessarily end in death, and death means the loss of these
charisms unless society makes some attempt to preserve them.
But the only way to keep them alive is to institutionalize
them. A fraternity, a society, an organization, an establishment dedicated to the memory of and preservation of the
principles of the person who was so significantly graced with
influential and valuable charismata keeps alive in the consciousness of men and continues to produce in society the
benefits that such gifts bestow upon the human race. But the
charisms so preserved are not really those of the founder or
inspirer of the organization. They have lost their personal
quality. They are linked to the great one of the past only by
memory and documentation, not by personal contact. In the
organization they tend to become abstract and absolute. They
lose their original human warmth. A passion for truth among
people reveals them for what they are, surrogate, institutionalized forms of what was once powerful, beautiful, human,
charismatic. *Corruptio optimi pessima.*

One would suspect that Nietzsche had the Christian Church
in mind when he proposed his idea of the ultimate devaluation
of the highest human values. For the New Testament makes
very clear that one of the central doctrines of Christianity is
that of the mystical identity between Christ and the believer.
The Pauline idea of the mystical body is one which captivated
the minds of many of the early Fathers of the Church and
formed the basis of their own theories of spirituality. Christ's
personal numinosity, his power, his goodness, his life, his
very being are in some mysterious way prolonged in time
and extended in space by the faithful. Because of their
belief they really live with his life, and so become a sign of
him in the world. His personal charisms are preserved in
them in the world because as a group, as a body of believers,
they are truly, if mysteriously and mystically, identified with
him. The heart of this mystery, of course, is found in the

idea that Christ retains his own personal unique identity, that which distinguished him as historical personage; so too do those individuals who identify themselves with him through faith: they remain exactly who they are as persons. The identity of which that faith speaks then is obviously achieved through some kind of union. Theology has insisted, though, right from the beginning that it is not merely some kind of moral union, that is, a union effected by intention or life-style such as exists in human societies like the Daughters of the American Revolution, or even more closely knit unities like the family. Nor on the other hand is it a physical union such as would exist between the cells or organs of a human body. The body analogy was the one used by St. Paul, but merely to distinguish the unique relationship of members of the Church to Christ and one another from membership in a purely human organization. The Church certainly was not conceived of by Paul in a purely physical way as a kind of monstrous superbody of Christ. No, the union which results in a kind of identity is purely spiritual, but nonetheless real; mysterious and mystical, but authentic and true. It is mysterious or mystical because it is quite unlike any other union. It lies somewhere in the middle on a continuum with moral union at one extreme and physical union at the other. The union or identity with Christ is achieved most perfectly in the whole group of believers. The whole organization is more fully representative of Christ than any individual or group of individuals in it. That is why it participates of the nature of a moral union such as characterizes voluntary human organizations. On the other hand, the bond of union with Christ and with one another is not, as in human voluntary organizations, intentional or psychological. It is not merely a common acceptance of principles of living, a common faith, or even the sharing of human love for Christ and one another. It is the physical reality of divine grace, of God's own love, which is his life, imparted to the members of this organization welding them together into a divinely human Christlike organism that until Omega day can be described only as a mystical body. That is why this organization participates in the nature of a physical union such as characterizes the components of living organisms, and perceives itself as radically different from any purely human voluntary organization.

As a surrogate of Christ, then, this organization, the Church, the mystical body of Christ, the people of God, devotes itself in the world not merely to the keeping alive of the memory of Christ and the preservation of his personal charisms, but to the very living of his life, and the continuation and perfection of his work. Of course, it is not really the very person of Christ; it is only his divinely established surrogate. Indeed it does not and cannot have his own personal charisms; to claim that would be blasphemy. It cannot see itself, as Christ did, having all power on heaven and earth; that is why it must live and feed upon its tradition. So to a certain extent Nietzsche's principle is valid: the charisms possessed by the Church are institutionalized forms of some of the personal charisms of Jesus, and as such cannot be valued as the charisms of Jesus himself. On the other hand, because the Church exists as an organization having a unique relationship to the one who inspired its establishment, Jesus, the charismatic devaluation which has occurred in it is not to be put on a level with that transpiring in purely human societies. In the latter truth and authenticity eventually overcome dedication and zeal and reveal a loss of both meaning and substance in the institutionalized charismata. In the Church, however, authentic faith suggests a retention of meaning and intent and an alteration and limitation only of modality in the institutionalized charisms of Jesus. Of course, there occurs a devaluation in the Church as well as in other societies in the sense that not all of the charisms of the founder or inspirer can be preserved. Some are so highly personal as completely to defy institutionalization or even memorialization.

The Church, of all organizations, then, stands in the best position to preserve not merely the abstract and objectified charismata of its inspirer, but in some sense his personhood as well. For only the Church (though to be sure other organizations have tried to imitate it) can appeal to the mysterious and the mystical; only the Church can claim divine institution. For the ancients who did not fully appreciate the uniqueness of personhood, the Church could be spoken of as Christ in the here and now. Even individual Christians who reflected the personal charisms of the Master less obviously than did the Church as a whole could be called other Christs. The principle of Nietzsche was much less in evidence in the understanding and writings of early Christianity than it is today when psychology has taught us the absolute uniqueness and individuality of the human person and his charisms and traits. We are much more tempted than our predecessors of eras long gone to interpret identifications of the Church, her ministers or members with Christ as metaphors. The fact, though, is that it is not merely a metaphor; nor on the other hand is it a literal declaration of objective personal identity. It can be seen only as the announcement of one of the deepest and most perplexing mysteries of our faith. But if it is not a metaphor, mysterious though it may be, what gives it a note of reality, a sound of authenticity? What in the concrete produces this quasi-identity? The New Testament gives an answer: the *charis* and certain of the *charismata* of Christ. The Church and at least some of its individual members assume an identity with Christ, can be called other Christs to the extent that they possess grace and certain of the charisms of Christ.

What does *charis* mean? What is grace? We have gone into this issue in detail in a former book entitled *A Contemporary Theology of Grace;* here we can only briefly limn an answer to these questions. Grace is God's loving presence and the transformation of human life in it. Grace is the very life of

Jesus to the extent that it reflected God's love (which is, as Scripture indicates, his very life) and the fullest and most total effect it can have upon a human being. Grace is the beauty of Jesus loving God and his fellow-men in the best way possible. Grace is the omnipotence of God crystallized in love. Grace is the figure, the character, the image, the imprint of the facies of the loving Jesus. It is his mysterious identity with the Father and with mankind achieved through love, which he shares with his fellow men. It is that divine love in the lives of men which transforms them into a living likeness of Jesus.

What does *charisma* mean? What is a charism? It is a gift given out of love to excite love, that is not itself love. It is a potential source of grace. Traditionally it has been defined as a special gift or privilege given by God to certain individuals not primarily for their own benefit and sanctification (this is the role of grace) but for the community, for the attainment of some salutary effect in others. It is an instrument, a tool, a medium opening the way to grace, to love. The New Testament mentions charisms that are quite extraordinary like the gifts of prophecy, speaking in or interpreting tongues, healing and discerning spirits, as well as those that are rather ordinary and appear as offices or jobs in the community, like serving as an apostle or teacher or ruler. The point, though, is that they are like grace itself (St. Thomas sees them as a kind of grace), freely bestowed as talents or special powers upon the individual by God himself. The community cannot or does not create them. It can only recognize them where they exist and affirm or approve of them as God-given. They are so highly personal that they cannot, apart from the direct action of God, be communicated or passed on to others, though their existence in those who possess them can be memorialized by the community.

The Church, then, maintains a mystical identity with Christ because of grace and because, through the promise of Christ and under divine guidance, it possesses in an authentic though institutionalized form certain of the personal charisms of the Master.

Priesthood is one of the charisms Jesus enjoyed. The New Testament applies the term "priest" in its fullest and strictest sense to him. That is, it is clear from the New Testament that the early Church regarded Christ as an authentic sacerdotal personage empowered by God to offer true ritual sacrifice and to perform an office of mediation between God and man. Jesus is as truly a priest as was Aaron or Melchizedek in the Old Testament; indeed, he is a priest in a fuller and more authentic sense than Aaron, Melchizedek or any other recognized priest. Though in the Gospels he nowhere proclaims himself to be a priest, he insinuates by figures and examples that the mission given him by his heavenly Father is a sacerdotal one. He speaks of his death as a sacrificial oblation for sin (Mark 10:45; 14:24). He views himself as mediating to man the true meaning of the law (Matthew 5:17–48). In the Gospel of John he presents himself as the revealer of the secrets of his heavenly Father. In the eyes of John, Christ's suffering and death form a sacred ritual for which he "consecrated himself" (17:19), that is, dedicated himself in priestly fashion for the benefit of the community. Jesus' prayer at the Last Supper is his priestly oblation marking his death as an act of expiation to God for the sins of men. The letters of St. Paul depict Jesus as a new lamb of sacrifice, a Passover victim opening up to Jew and Gentile alike the possibility of escaping servitude to guilt and sin and attaining to the true freedom of justification. The most explicit treatment of the priesthood of Jesus is the one set forth in the Epistle to the Hebrews. Jesus, more effectively than Aaron and his line, has intervened with God on behalf of sinners, and through his sacrifice of himself not only has won everlasting glory for himself as priest and mediator, but also has made it possible for men to live in a state of true holiness.

The Epistle to the Hebrews indicates that the source of Jesus' priesthood lay not in any anointing or consecration by human hands, but in the fact that, being at one and the same time both the Son of God and true man, by his very nature he is constituted in a unique way the perfect mediator and consequently the priest par excellence. Down through the centuries theologians have seen in this avowal an intimation that in Jesus the charism of priesthood is really identified with the full and most perfect possession of grace he enjoys by virtue of the hypostatic union, with the *gratia capitis.*

If as we have said the Christian community maintains the identity with Jesus suggested by the New Testament through its possession of grace and certain charisms of the Master, we might well suspect that one of those charisms is Jesus' priestly one. Our suspicion is borne out by New Testament teaching. The Christian people are called a priestly people. The sacerdotal appellations of Christ are applied to them in the selfsame language. Though the words of Jesus as we have them in the New Testament do not directly claim priestly functions for his followers any more than they do for himself, one can easily infer that such a role is hinted at. Jesus' disciple has to take up his cross of sacrifice every day and follow in the footsteps of the Master (Matthew 16:24f.). To participate in the reward that Jesus promises, his follower has to drink of the cup of which he drank, presumably the cup of sacrifice (Matthew 20:22). He has also to mediate the good news of salvation to his fellows (Luke 9:60, 10:1ff.). St. Paul considers both the faith and monetary offerings of the Christian as an oblation of sacrifice (Philippians 2:17; 4:18). The true follower of Jesus is one who continuously offers his body as a sacrificial victim in a truly spiritual rite of faith (Romans 12:1). Of course First Peter 2:5–9 offers the most explicit and best-known reference: the people of God must consider themselves as a chosen race, a royal priesthood empowered to render homage and spiritual sacrifices to God through the action of Jesus.

It takes only a little analysis to see how already here the principle of Nietzsche is operative. Though the same terms are applied to it as were applied in the New Testament to the priesthood of Christ, the Church's endowment is not really the personal sacerdotal charism of Christ, but only a participation in it. The highest value has to be devaluated when it is transferred from Christ to his Church.

The modality of the priestly charism existing in the Christian community is radically different from the modality of the charism in Christ himself, though the meaning and intent are the same, and so reflect Christ in his people. First, the Epistle to the Hebrews clearly teaches that Christ's sacrifice has been offered once and for all; it need not and cannot be repeated in the modality in which Christ executed it. Secondly, the priestly charism which the Church enjoys does not emanate from its constitution as a following or discipleship of Christ. It has to originate in the will of Christ to keep the memory of himself fresh among his followers not merely through word of mouth and writings but in the unique way of imparting, to the extent that he could, his own grace and charisms. It is in this sense that we truly say of Christ that he instituted the sacrament of orders; Christ was constituted priest, as the Epistle to the Hebrews indicates, by his very nature as God-man; the Church has a priestly charism like that of Christ because Christ willed his disciples to take up their cross and follow him, to imitate him as an apprentice imitates the master, to drink of his cup, to follow the ritual he observed in memory of him. Thirdly, the Church soon discovered that, in her, the priestly charism is not identified with grace as it was in Christ. Christ's charismatic gifts are all really identified with one another and with grace because of his God-manhood. In the Church charisms are separable from one another as well as from grace, which heralds the sanctifying presence of the Lord in a deeper and more radical sense. Finally, the sacerdotal charism of the Church, obviously exists in an institutionalized form, whereas that of Christ was personal. The institutional charism as such remains to a certain extent under the control of the institution. True, whatever is its essence cannot be changed: it must forever reflect the priestly charism of Christ, and so render him present as priest in the community. Then too, its fixed modality as determined by the will of Christ cannot be altered: it can never be made a personal power for the aggrandizement of the one who possesses it. But otherwise, seemingly, its use, manifestation and operation are under the direction of the institution upon which it has been bestowed by Christ.

Apart from the case of Christ and the people of God as a whole, the New Testament does not attribute the priestly charism to anyone or any group. As we have indicated, it takes note of other charisms of Christ or his Spirit in the Church at large, such as that of love and concern for the poor, as well as in certain privileged persons or groups in the Church, such as the gift of prophecy or speaking in tongues. Some of these charisms obviously originate because of the special action of the Spirit of Jesus on those who receive them. One does not say: "Lord, Jesus!" except through the Spirit, much less speak in tongues. Others of these charisms are natural gifts, native abilities or talents that people possess or cultivate; these are recognized by the community and put to good use by the Spirit. Such are the charisms of leadership or governing and teaching.

In addition to charisms the New Testament recognizes numerous offices or jobs set up by the Church for the service of the community. Only one such office seems to have been established by Christ himself, that of apostle; as a creation of Christ the apostleship seemed also to have carried with it certain charisms. But it would seem to be the only office that participates also of the nature of a charism.

Notable among these offices in the early Christian community was that of ministry, or service of the people. The New Testament does not apply the word "priestly" to this office, or even to the office of apostle. The first ministers seemed to have been the deacons, who were set up by the apostles to take charge of some of the corporeal works of mercy in the community. A later structural system of the churches acknowledges the existence of overseers and elders who seem also to have been recognized by the community as ministers. The overseer, supervisor or bishop had as his task invigilation, the modeling of the ideal Christian life and governance, as is clear from the pastoral epistles. From the profile given he emerges definitively as an administrative officer. The elder, or rather the elders, for the term is usually used in the plural, are a much more mysterious lot. The elders or presbyters (from which our word "priest" is derived) apparently constituted some kind of board of advisers for the community and perhaps for the supervisor of the community. Sometimes the word "presbyter" is interchangeable with "overseer."

How it happened no one can be sure, for there is a dearth of documentation, but the fact is certain. In the course of time the priestly charism of the Church began to be personified in the office holders, in particular in the offices of supervisor (bishop), elder (priest) and deacon. Perhaps in the post-Testamental period the Church began to realize in practice what Nietzsche formulated into a principle centuries later: to institutionalize is to devaluate. There was a need to see charism alive and at work in persons. And the extraordinary charisms of Testamental times were on the wane; what remained was only the institutionalized sacerdotal charism of the Church itself. Presumably through the will of the community expressed through those responsible for its welfare this charism, originating in the person of Christ himself, was now re-personified in the officeholders of the time, and eventually attached to the office itself.

Whether this theory is true or not is, of course, given the lack of adequate documentation, largely conjectural, but it does seem to accord with universal human behavior. People respond to the concrete more readily than to the abstract, to persons more readily than to institutions, to voiced commands more readily than to written principles. A priesthood that was too institutional, too abstract, too gnostic, too universal would eventually prove to be an ineffectual one. Even the Christian needed a priest he could see. There is some hint of this Church order, of a partial completion of the identification of priestly charism with episcopal office at least, in the writings of Clement of Rome; the process may have been under way then, even in late Testamental times, but certainly it was in full spate by the end of the second century.

Howsoever the repersonification of the priesthood may have been accomplished very early in the history of the Church, one thing is certain: it posed no threat to the New Testament teaching. The Church as a community was still regarded as in primary possession of the priestly charism. The officeholder participated in it only to the extent that his ministerial duties to the community required. It would seem then that he possessed it precisely as a representative of the whole Church to the particular community he served. He possessed it as an agent, as a chargé d'affaires, as a legate of the Church at large. The charism he was acknowledged to possess was not, to be sure, his own; he was not a priest in his own right. It was the priestly charism of Christ institutionalized in his Church. So when Augustine baptized, it was really Christ who baptized. When John Chrysostom pronounced the words of Christ at the Last Supper in the Holy Synaxis, it was really Christ who pronounced them. Here then is the essence of the priestly charism as possessed by a minister in the Church: he is a member empowered to represent the whole community at large, and, within the limits of his office, to speak for that community and commit it to the exercise of its priestly charism, and to bring to bear its sacerdotal operation on the person or persons to whom he is ministering. He is like a minister of state who can speak for his government officially to individual citizens or groups of citizens. He is a true representive of the Church, rendering its sacerdotal charism present in his person to those to whom he ministers. He becomes a personification of the Church insofar as it possesses a priestly charism. He is the personal agent of Christ's sacerdotal power inasmuch as it is possessed by his Church.

There are some charisms like intelligence that individuals possess by native endowment or training. There are others like leadership that are discovered because they are recognized by people in general. There are other charisms like saintliness that are the result of the special operation of the Holy Spirit. The Church has never claimed that these charisms, howsoever desirable they might be in a bishop or priest, are conferred by ordination. If the Church wants ministers who are intelligent, saintly and capable of leading men, she must seek out those who are so endowed and ordain them.

The priestly charism which the Church can bestow has to be the one it possesses: the institutionalized charism of Christ's sacerdotal power. This charism has to be imparted as it exists in the Church without modification or change or purpose or intent, and once bestowed, it has to capacitate the one ordained to act in virtue of it. True, the impartation of it can imply some limitation of its extent; that is, each representative is not necessarily empowered to use every facet and aspect of the total charism. But it cannot imply curtailment of contact with the elements of the charism over which he has dominion, for these really belong to the Church itself and evidence in it the priestly mission of Christ himself.

In this theory, then, the essence of the priesthood resides in a very simple reality: the empowering of a member of the Church officially to represent it vis-à-vis the priestly charism imparted to it by the will of Christ. A priest then may simply be defined as <u>an ambassador of the Church to his fellow Christians.</u>

To be sure, the fact that the Church's priestly charism can be communicated in a special way to some of its members does not imply that it is lost in the Church at large. Apart from the ministerial or official priesthood there is a common priesthood in which all Christians share. From New Testament times on the Church has always professed this doctrine. And theologians have taught that this common priesthood comes to the individual member of the Church through his reception of the sacrament of baptism initially, and that it is perfected and brought to completion through the reception of the sacrament of confirmation. It is always necessary to distinguish this common priesthood of the faithful from the ministerial priesthood about which this essay is principally concerned. Pius XII in his allocution *Magnifcate Dominum* of November 2, 1954, clearly states: "The priesthood of the laity, profound and mysterious as it is, differs not in degree, but in essence from the priesthood properly so called." We would see this essential difference properly maintained in the theory we have just propounded. The ordained priest is called to be an *official* representative and witness of the Church's priestly charism, while the lay priest is only a *de facto* witness. The ordained priest can in the prescribed forms speak in the name of the whole Church and commit it to action in a given situation; the lay priest can act and speak only in his own name as an individual, private Christian. True, both can act in a priestly way; both can in their own words and actions reflect Christ's own priesthood. But the minister does it in a public, official way; the lay person privately, on his own. Thus an American citizen living in a foreign country may by his exemplary conduct win the admiration of the people of this land for the United States; he may be instrumental in promoting peace and goodwill. No one will deny that his action is effective and in the best interests of his country. But if he is only a private citizen he cannot commit the United States government, which represents the whole people, to a peace treaty with this foreign country. He is not an official, but only a private representative of the people of the United States. The American ambassador alone, of all the United States citizens in that country, can act for the people of the United States. If he were to sign a peace treaty with the government of that country the whole people of the United States and their government would be committed to honor it, for the ambassador is empowered under certain conditions to act for the government he represents. He can speak for his government and commit it to action; no private citizen can do this. This is certainly an essential difference, the difference in the way of acting of the official representative, the ambassador, and the private citizen. So too there is an essential difference in the operation of the ministerial and lay priesthood in the theory we have proposed. This is not to belittle or denigrate the common priesthood. The priestly charism of the Church is very much in evidence in the lives of the laity; indeed, at times it has shone forth much more brilliantly in the lives of the faithful than it has in those of ministers. The layman too is anointed by the Spirit, and the Spirit can and does speak in and through him. But the fact is that he is not sacramentally deputed or commissioned by the Church to act officially in its name.

The normal way for the Church to communicate its priestly charism to those who are to be made its official agents is through sacramental ordination. The matter and form of this sacrament, since they were not explicitly determined by Christ, have always remained subject to the Church's own selection. Only in rather recent times did Pope Pius XII settle a longstanding theological dispute about the matter and fix definitely the words that were to be considered the form in the administration of this sacrament at its various levels. If an objection is lodged against the priesthood as ambassadorial service on

behalf of the Church on the grounds that a layman could be
delegated by the community or its chief representative to
speak for it in some way, or act for it in some official capacity,
we would have to answer in this way. If the deputation were
truly in the area of priestly activity, in the area of ecclesial
operation governed by the Church's sacerdotal charism, then
that deputation, no matter what form was used, if made by
the proper authority, that is, the pope (who alone could do
such a thing), then it would have to be considered as tanta-
mount to ordination; the deputation would take place through
the sacrament of orders, given by the supreme authority in the
Church a new form and new matter in this instance. If, however, it was a deputation to act in the name of the Church in
some other area, obviously there would be no problem.

A second objection to the theory we have proposed springs
from the fact that it seems to reverse the usual conception of
the distribution of power and authority in the Church. It
makes the Church look too democratic, whereas it cannot be.
From the earliest times authority was concentrated in the
Roman pontiff and the monarchical bishops, not in the Church
at large, and this authority sprang from the sacerdotal
charism. This view, which was the prevalent one before Vatican II, conceives of priesthood as initially given to only a few,
and like a leaven, eventually spreading through the mass without losing its concentration in the original yeast. Our theory,
however, would see priesthood as initially dispersed throughout the whole mass, and eventually concentrating itself in certain areas. Though this is a good objection we think that our
theory better corresponds to what we now know about Church
order in New Testament times. If the pre-Vatican II view
were true, we might logically expect the term "priest" to be
applied to the apostles, the overseers and the elders, and not
merely to Christ and the Church at large. If the theory that
we have proposed gives the impression that the priest is
merely the delegate of the community, this certainly is not

intended. The priest receives his charism, which is a participation in the Church's own, through the medium and ministration of those who already possess it. Though there have been a few cases in which the principle of *oikonomia* (that is, a direct designation of a minister by a community without ordination since it is impossible to obtain a person properly qualified to ordain) was applied, the normal and traditional way of imparting the priestly charism is through ordination; thus the priestly power comes from God himself in the sacramental ritual. But it is radically a power to speak on behalf of the community, to use the mediating power of the community with God and to activate the charisms promised by Christ to his Church. This power must be seen as belonging to the whole community of the faithful, which as Vatican II indicates is actually the Church, in the first instance, but administered by the leaders of the community who already possess the priestly charism in the fullest measure.

The charism of the priest, according to our theory, is a participation in the sacerdotal charism of the Church. The charism of the Church, in turn, is the institutionalized priestly charism of Christ himself. Now we must ask just what in the concrete that priestly charism of Christ is that the Church possesses under a different modality. The best answer given to that question in our time, we believe, is the one proposed by Father Joseph Lécuyer in his book *Le sacerdoce dans le mystère du Christ* (Paris, Cerf, 1957: *Lex orandi*, 24). Christ had a twofold task as priest: that of reconciling sinful man with God, and that of uniting men with God and one another in love. He accomplished this task by means of two religious mysteries which form the essence of his priestly ministry: the paschal mystery and the pentecostal mystery.

The paschal mystery is the mystery of reconciliation. It is the mystery of death and resurrection. It is the paradox of achieving the transcendence of humanity through acceptance of it. It is the mystery of Christ's sacrifice precisely as an act of expiation, of his resurrection to a new and better life, of his disappearance from earth in order to entrust his followers with the task of completing his work. It is the mystery of passing into light through darkness. It is the mystery of the power of sin and the victory of grace. It is the mystery of the passage from slavery to freedom. It is precisely the personal mystery of Christ, the Son of God in his flesh, the anointed one, the divine athlete who has overcome the world.

The pentecostal mystery is the mystery of love. Jesus accomplished the paschal mystery because of love. The pentecostal mystery is the mystery that lies behind, that is apprehended at the root of, the paschal mystery. It is the mystery of the coming and indwelling of the Spirit of God. It is the mystery of wisdom and union. It is the mystery of God's abiding gift of himself to men. It is the mystery of divine counseling and comforting. It is the mystery of total dedication of self to the community. It is the mystery that lies behind all the divine charisms given for the edification of the people of God. It is the personal mystery of the Spirit of Jesus, the advocate, the consoler, the guide and ruler of Christ's flock.

Mircea Eliade has written: "One becomes truly a man only by conforming to the teaching of the myths, that is by imitating the gods." Only in Christianity is this primitive idea realizable. Christ has bestowed his priestly charism upon the Church so that in it the paschal and pentecostal mysteries may not only be commemorated, but re-enacted and relived, so that the Church might have an identity with him in his priestly function. While it was the priestly task of Jesus to set forth and accomplish and fulfill these mysteries in his life, it is that of his Church to memorialize them, act them out again and fill up what is still lacking in them because of the defects of man. This is then precisely the task of the priesthood in the Church, of the ministerial priesthood on the official, ambassadorial level, and of the common priesthood on the individual, private level.

There has been a long tradition in the Church supporting this view of the paschal and pentecostal mysteries as the central theme of priestly activity. Father Lécuyer presents at length in his book the historical and theological arguments. But the notion is also set forth in a way that all, at least at one time in the history of the Church, could comprehend. It is set forth in symbols that even one who is not a theologian, provided that he understand the symbolism, can appreciate.

In baptism and confirmation, the two sacraments of the common priesthood, and in two parts of the sacraments of orders, ordination of a priest of the second order and of a bishop, use is made of oil. Two different kinds of oil are used in the various rituals, olive oil called oil of the catechumens, and a sweet-smelling balsam oil called chrism. In the ancient world olive oil was considered to be a great source of energy. The athlete applied it to his muscles before entering a contest. The early Church appreciated the fact that the mystery of reconciliation, the mystery of death and resurrection, involved a tremendous struggle with self. For this superhuman strength was needed. So this oil became the symbol of the paschal mystery. Balsam oil served well as a deodorant or perfume. It was often used by prominent officials who had to appear often in public. This was the kind of oil that was poured over the heads of kings and priests to indicate that one who carried a public charge ought not be offensive to the people they served. Their lives ought to have a sweet smell about them, not the stench of corruption and venality. For the Christian, life's sweetness came from love; love was what made it possible for people to live close to one another without offense. So balsam oil or chrism became the symbol of the pentecostal mystery.

The two grades or steps of the lay priesthood, the private or non-official witnessing of the charism of Jesus, are distinguished according to their power of representing principally either the paschal or pentecostal mystery. The paschal mystery chiefly is relived in baptism, and the pentecostal mystery primarily is celebrated in confirmation. The baptized Christian goes forth to proclaim the work of reconciliation that has been effected in him. Christ is witnessed in his conversion, in his living of the new life. The confirmed Christian, on the other hand, is urged through the charisms of the Spirit he has received to work actively in love and out of love to communicate that Spirit to others for the building up of the body of Christ that is his Church.

Similarly on the level of the ministerial priesthood there are two stages of involvement corresponding to the paschal and pentecostal mysteries. The priest of the second order is principally the agent of the Church's work of reconciliation. His essential task is to experience, to celebrate and relive the paschal mystery in the name of the Christian community. The bishop, on the other hand, is the official agent additionally and chiefly of the pentecostal mystery. He must be not only the symbol but the effecter of unity in the flock. His charity must be perfect. His very life must be poured out like balm upon the body he is pledged to support and unify by his consecration in the Spirit.

The Church strengthens the lay priest by anointing him with olive oil when in the sacrament of baptism it strengthens him to undergo and display in his life the paschal mystery. So too it prepares with that same oil its official representative of the paschal mystery, the priest of the second order, for the death and resurrection he must experience if indeed his priestly life is an imitation of the sacrifice he celebrates at the altar. And as it places the soothing and sweet-smelling balsam oil on the head of those who are sealed in love by the Spirit, so the Church anoints the head of the new bishop with the oil of consolation, so that, enkindled by the Spirit, this priest of the first order might unite the people of God by his wisdom and cherish them with the perfection of his love.

The Church's priestly charism, then, is parceled out among its members so that through their collaboration all might become a sign of unity and a witness to the world. But on the level of ministerial priesthood, of official representation of that charism, there stands a third order which of itself reflects neither the paschal nor pentecostal mysteries. It is the order of deacon. The concrete aspect of the Church's sacerdotal charism that is displayed in the diaconate is one that forms the groundwork, the opening up to, the preparation for the reliving of the paschal and pentecostal mysteries. Before he brought these mysteries into being in his own priestly life Jesus announced his intent in creating them. They would serve mankind in a way no other philosophy, no other religion, no other human endeavor has. Through them Jesus will fulfill the promise that the Chosen One of God would be a true servant of mankind. It is precisely Christ's ministry, his service of humanity, the prelude to and foundation of the paschal and pentecostal mysteries, that forms the heart of the deacon's priestly charism. The deacon witnesses, proclaims and reflects service, servanthood, in the Church. The dynamic of his priestly existence is precisely that of ministry, of service of man in every need and difficulty and problem of his earthly life. To be sure, the deacon, as one who is baptized and confirmed, also is involved with the paschal and pentecostal mysteries; but only as a layman is. His official priestly task, his ambassadorial role, lies in the area of service. In the Gospel of John, after uttering his high-priestly prayer, prior to his celebration of and inauguration of the paschal and pentecostal mysteries, Jesus donned an apron and performed his first ritual act. He washed the feet of his disciples. Through this human service he opened the way to mystery. Here he foreshadowed the priestly task of the deacon in his Church.

A story is told about a recent pope's being questioned about

how he would define priesthood. "A priest is," he is supposed
to have replied, "whatever I choose to make him." These words
certainly would cause no conflict with the theory of the priesthood we have been elaborating. If the essence of priesthood
rests in being an official agent of the Church in certain areas
of its mission to the world, then it is indeed a flexible tool in
the hands of those charged with the accomplishment of that
mission. The traditions of the past have indeed preserved and
fostered that essence; but it is not likely that the decisions of
the future, provided that the Church does remain always conscious of its priestly mission, will lose or destroy it, no matter
how radical they seem. For the priest can always be priest as
long as he can, through the sacerdotal charism of the Church
whose ambassador he is, render present in the world Christ
and his life-giving mysteries.

CHAPTER III

Women as Priests

The post-Vatican II era has already been dubbed by some as the "ecumenical age." More serious attempts have been made in this period to effect some kind of co-operation between Christian churches than at any time since shortly after the Reformation was launched by Martin Luther. The road to real unity, of course, will be a very difficult one indeed, and one of the chief obstacles that will be encountered will always be the theological issue of priesthood and ministry. Different churches have varied views of ministry, many of which the Roman Catholic Church cannot accept. It is amazing, however, how well the theological spadework that might eventually lead to a recognition of Anglican orders by the Catholic Church has proceeded. The ultimate decision, however, will have to take into account a fact that is becoming increasingly significant from a theological and pastoral standpoint. The Anglican Church now has women priests.

For many years certain Protestant churches both in Europe and America have been ordaining women to the ministry. Although Reformed Judaism employed female rabbis in Germany for some time, the first American was assigned to an New York synagogue in 1972. It is only natural then that Catholic women's groups are manifesting concern about the

possibility of women priests. While the attitude of the Church
in the not too remote past has been most negative, there are
some signs of relaxation in the legislation prohibiting women
to function in an official capacity in the Church. While women
still are interdicted from serving Mass at the altar, they may
now stand in the sanctuary when acting as commentators or
leaders of song. The most significant breakthrough, of course,
has occurred in the fact that now women are accepted along
with lay men as distributors of holy Communion in parishes
which lack sufficient clergy.

The theory of priesthood which we have expounded in the
previous chapter sets no limitation of sex upon the Church's
ministers. Qualified women as well as men could become representatives of the Church and witnesses of the ministry and
mysteries of Christ in the various orders. In fact, the sacerdotal
charism of a Church which is spoken of traditionally in feminine terms might be better personalized in a woman than in a
man. Indeed, there can be no doubt that even in the present
situation women are more likely than men to exercise and
perfect their common priestly roles. It is usually the Catholic
mother who mediates the faith to her children, inspires the
family to pray and sets a good example both in home and
parish religious activities. Her common priestly role is so
often *de facto* more significant in the Church than the official
operation of ordained ministers.

But the decision that will have eventually to be made by
ecclesiastical authorities will be influenced by factors other
than theological theory. The role expectation of the minister
from the standpoint of the laity will be an important consideration. Where they are employed, women commentators and
distributors of Communion have not, as some predicted, been
rejected; in fact, they seem to have been warmly welcomed.
But the rejection of women priests in certain highly conservative quarters of the Church certainly looms as an unhappy
possibility until there is sufficient support by the Church as

a whole and adequate instruction. But an even more important factor, since we are a traditional Church, and past
policy is more important in decision-making than theological
theory, is the history of the question. Have there ever been
women priests in the past?

It is a fact that women were ordained to the ministry in
the Church, if not from New Testament times, at least from
the immediate post-Testamental period down to the eighteenth
century. Despite what St. Thomas and those who have simply
parroted him have taught, there is, as we shall see, good
reason to believe that these women, at least in certain times
and places, were as really and truly ordained as men were.
Though as time went on the practice of ordaining women
became more restricted where and when it did occur, it seems
to have been acknowledged as valid by the Church universal.
It is astounding, but nonetheless true, that in the early Church,
besides incontrovertible evidence for the existence of deaconesses, there are sources referring to the feminine counterparts
of priests and bishops.

The pertinent New Testament texts come from the letters
of St. Paul. Two times he applies the Greek word meaning
"deacon" to women. To be sure, there is no absolute certainty
that in his use of this word he would imply that deaconesses
would be ordained and perform functions in the Church reserved to the order of deacons in later times. But there is no
reason to believe that the male deacons mentioned in Acts and
elsewhere would either. The most celebrated text is that of
Romans 16:1: "I commend to you our sister Phoebe, who is
deaconess in the church of Cenchrae [a small port near
Corinth]." The Greek text reads: "*ousan diakonon tēs
ekklēsias tēs en Kegxreais.*" Many English translators describe Phoebe in a completely uncontroversial way as a "helper
in the church at Cenchrae" (Goodspeed); or as a woman
"who is in the ministry of the church at Cenchrae" (Con-
fraternity); or again as one who "has devoted her services to

the church at Cenchrae" (Knox). But the Kleist-Lilly translation and the Jerusalem Bible acknowledge Phoebe as a
deaconess of the church at Cenchrae. C. K. Barrett in his *The
Epistle to the Romans* in Harper's New Testament Com-
mentaries, although he is not certain about the use of the
word when it is applied to women, is of the opinion that
the word *diakonos* was on its way to being applied in a
technical sense by the time this epistle was written (c. A.D.
55). The fact is that in this text the selfsame word in its
feminine form (*hē diakonos*) is employed by Paul to describe
Phoebe's connection with the church at Cenchrae as is employed by him to designate the male helpers of the bishops in
other churches (*ho diakonos,* for example in Philippians 1:1
and First Timothy 3:8, 12). At any rate the text announces
that Phoebe was going to Rome, perhaps on some official business: some exegetes surmise that the "business" of Phoebe
was the delivery of Paul's letter to the community at Rome.
Whether it was or not is by no means certain; perhaps no
official work of ministry is implied at all. Paul merely asks the
faithful at Rome to receive her kindly, not merely because she
is a Christian, but one with a special claim on the charity of all
since she has been a benefactress to many, including Paul
himself.

In First Timothy 3:8ff. Paul enumerates traits desired in
those who are to assume the office of deacon, which obviously
was considered an important charge in the Church order of
the time. In verse 11 he shifts his attention to women, and
seems to require in them the same admirable qualities. It
does not appear likely that he is talking about women in
general in this context; he has already discussed women in
general in chapter 2, verses 9–15. He seems to be referring to
a special class of women, as the connective word *hōsautōs*
might well indicate. There could likely be question here of
women whose role in the Church parallels that of the deacons.
This would explain most logically why they must be graced

with the same virtues. St. Thomas Aquinas and many other
commentators believe that Paul was laying down directives
for the wives of the deacons: they had to be graced with the
same qualities as their husbands to be acceptable to the
community. Other commentators on this passage, however,
reject this interpretation because the phrase lacks any pos-
sessive connector like *gunaikas autōn,* their women. In his
eleventh Homily on First Timothy St. John Chrysostom un-
equivocally applies this text to deaconesses.

Another text that merits consideration is First Timothy
5:9–13. It is concerned with the question of the election of
widows in the Church. There is no doubt that the Christian
community from the beginning felt itself obliged to pension
and support destitute widows. The text of First Timothy certainly is concerned with this work of chairty, at least obliquely.
However, some scholars are not willing to admit that this is
the primary or only significance of the passage. They appeal
to the fact that the charity of the Christian community, in
accordance with the directives of Christ himself, could not be
conditioned. The early Christian community must have apprehended the gist of the Gospel relative to the care of the poor
and destitute: no requirements were to be demanded by the
community on the part of recipients of its largesse of charity.
Alms were to be given freely without regard to person. So
these exegetes deny that this passage refers merely to the community's concern for widows in general. They imply that here
again there is question of a special group of widows chosen
for some definite role in the community. Just what that role
in the concrete might be is, again, unfortunately not explained.
But from the list of qualifications some commentators have
opined that Paul is dealing here again with the criteria to be
used by overseers like Timothy in selecting deaconesses to assist them in ministry to women.

Indications that there may have been deaconesses in the
Church even in New Testament times are scanty and by no

means certain in the Scriptures themselves. A more plausible argument can be made for their existence in the early years of the second century, however, from a reference in Pliny the Younger's famous letter to the Emperor Trajan inquiring how to treat the Christians. In his communication Pliny admits having tortured two Christian female servants (*ancillis*), who, as he says, are called deaconesses (*ministrae*) in order to get some better information on what Christianity is all about. Why he chose these women is not clear, but perhaps he felt that, because of their sex, they would be more prone to yield to his wishes under torture, and because they held a position of responsibility in the community, he would be able to get from them a more complete and authentic explanation of Christian beliefs.

At any rate it is certain from such documents as the *Apostolic Tradition* of Hippolytus, the *Apostolic Constitutions*, the *Didascalia* or *Catholic Teaching of the Apostles*, the *Testament of Our Lord* and the *Apostolic Church Order* as well as the works of some of the Fathers like Tertullian and Epiphanius that deaconesses did exist very early in the history of the Church. It would seem to be certain that the order was well established in some places at least by the beginning of the third century.

An examination of some of these documents reveals the role of the deaconesses in the community to be analogous to that of the deacons. As in the case of their male counterparts, theirs was a service-oriented work in the churches in which their order had been established. They were to make the rounds visiting the poor in their homes. They were especially enjoined to take care of sick women in the community. They served as intermediaries between the bishop and the female members of his flock. They were called upon to watch over and instruct catechumens of their own sex. They had to preside over the necessary examinations when virgins were accused of violation of their vow. Some of them were assigned to preside over the women's section of the assembly at liturgical gatherings. They had to guard the church doors against entry by women who were not members of the Christian community. They had the duty of preparing the bodies of the faithful for burial. Above all, however, they were called upon to assist in the baptism of adult women converts.

Undoubtedly this last function, assistance in the baptism of women, was their most important liturgical task, and an important reason for the foundation of their order in the Church in the first place. As is well known, in the early Church those to be baptized entered the pool or stream naked. According to the *Apostolic Tradition* of Hippolytus one or more deacons accompanied the men down into the water. The deacon asked each candidate: "Do you believe in God, the Father almighty?" And when he received the response: "I believe," he laid his hand upon the head of the catechumen and plunged him into the water for the first time. A similar procedure was followed when the candidate made his response to the second question about Jesus, his incarnation, death, resurrection, ascension and second coming at the end of time. Once again this was the order observed when the answer was received to the third inquiry about the Holy Spirit, the Church and the resurrection of all flesh.

Although Hippolytus makes no distinction between men and women in discussing baptism, we must presume that the deaconesses performed for the women what the deacons did for the men. The deacons and deaconesses for their respective sex also assisted in the anointing of the candidates for baptism. The initial anointing of women with the oil of exorcism seems to have been begun by a priest who applied it to the forehead of the candidate. But the anointing was later completed by the deaconesses, for, as we are told, it was extended to the whole body and all its members. By themselves the deaconesses anointed the newly baptized women with the oil of thanksgiving. They also outfitted the women with their white garments and presented them to the bishop for what the later Church would regard as confirmation. During this ceremony the oil of thanksgiving was once again applied to the head only of the newly baptized person. So it could be taken care of by the bishop alone for both male and female converts.

It might be surprising to learn that the teaching functions of the deaconesses were of special concern to and received great emphasis by early Christian writers. Certainly St. Paul had enjoined women to remain silent in church and to maintain an attitude of submissiveness. And the Fathers of the Church took this advice seriously indeed! But they did not interpret it to mean that those women who became official ministers of the Church, the deaconesses, should not assume any teaching role. They merely warned that women were not to presume to teach men: on the contrary their educative role was to be exercised only in regard to women, and this work was to be strictly supervised by the male clergy. The *Apostolic Constitutions* reveal a number of strictures placed upon female teachers. They are cautioned not to give quick and impulsive answers. They are warned to answer only as much as is necessary, no more. And they are enjoined to be particularly cautious and circumspect when essaying to explain the mysteries of the faith. Questions which they feel they are not prepared or able to answer should be remanded to the bishops. But we must not give the impression that all is negative in the early period of the existence of the order. Tertullian openly defends the right of these women to teach in the Church. He refutes those who would tend to exaggerate or distort the Pauline injunction: women should not speak in church, but this does not mean that they have to be silent everywhere. Apparently means of learning theology, apart from the strictly male schools, were available, because the Fourth Council of Carthage required perfect knowledge of everything pertaining to their ministry of any woman, be she virgin or widow, seeking admission into the order of deaconesses.

Outside of baptism, did the female clergy have any liturgical function? There are reasons to believe that they did. In early Christian funeral inscriptions a technical term is used to describe the relationship of a deceased bishop or priest to a given church: *sedit*. He is said to have sat or presided over the worship of the community. Today we say that a bishop has a see. This word is derived from the Latin *sedes*, the presidential chair. It too describes his relationship to the church to which he has been assigned. Now in the early Church in funeral inscriptions the same term that is used for bishops and priests is also applied to certain deceased widows. The implication is that these widows were also considered as ministers in the community and had a chair in the assembly similar to the bishop's. Sisto Scaglia in his *Notiones archaeologiae christianae* comes to this conclusion from his extensive examination of funeral inscriptions. In the various Christian communities widows were not merely held in special honor and regard outside of the assembly; it would seem that they even presided over the women's sections during the liturgy in chairs quite like the bishop's *cathedra*. The *Corpus Inscriptionum*, an extensive collection of Christian epitaphs from ancient times published at Berlin in 1905, gives a number of examples of such inscriptions found on or near the burial places of widows. In his *De virginibus velandis* Tertullian also mentions such a widow's seat. Indeed, in arguing against the propriety of second marriages, he appeals to the custom of the Church in not allowing women who have been married twice to be ordained (*allegi in ordinem*) or to preside (*praesidere*) in the community.

In two of these funeral inscriptions, one from Terni, and the other from the basilica of St. Praxedes in Rome dating from the time of Pope Paschal I (ninth century), the very word *episcopa* (bishopess) is applied apropos of widows.

To be sure, the prohibitions which began to be proliferated in later times are indicative of the fact that widows and deaconesses associated themselves in more and more intimate ways with the very service of the altar. In the Nestorian church deaconesses ministered the sacred bread and the chalice to female communicants. The Monophysites permitted them also to preside over public prayer, to offer incense, and to present the bread and wine at the altar during the liturgy. But these practices were generally regarded both in Rome and Constantinople as encroachments upon the prerogatives of the male clergy. The decree of Gratian carries a prohibition, attributed to Pope Soter, restraining ordained women or women religious from touching the sacred vessels or incensing the altar. The *Didascalia* as well as the *Apostolic Constitutions* warn women against preaching in a holy place, entering into theological disputations, serving at the altar and performing baptisms on their own authority. St. Epiphanius rants against those who would extend the ministry of the deaconesses to include strictly sacerdotal functions. On the other hand, the *Testament of Our Lord* implies that deaconesses regularly carried the Eucharist to women who were unable to attend church because they were sick at home.

When we come to consider the necessary requisites for acceptance into the order of deaconess, we are confronted with the difficult problem of relating this order to the state of widowhood. Was the order of deaconess in the earliest times reserved for specially qualified widows, or were other women admitted as well? It would seem that in some places the norms that St. Paul laid down for widows were applied in selecting candidates for the order of deaconess. They had to be widows, married only once, at least sixty years old, of good reputation, hospitable, charitable and devoted to service of the community. Tertullian, writing early in the third century, seems to have used the terms "widow" and "deaconess" interchangeably. In his *De virginibus velandis* he mentions that he had heard of a virgin who was not yet twenty years of age being accepted into the widowhood. Then again in his work *Ad uxorem* he apparently is referring to the order of deaconesses when he speaks of the priestly character of the widowhood (*sacerdotium viduitatis*). Even earlier, in the second century, St. Ignatius of Antioch appears to take note of a similiar phenomenon when in his letter to the Church at Smyrna he refers to "virgins who are enrolled among the widows." Such language becomes intelligible only if we understand that these writers use the word "widowhood" in a purely technical sense, applying it most likely to the order of deaconesses.

Other sources lead us to believe that not all those listed among the widows of certain communities were in fact distaff deacons. This would seem logical, because quite obviously not all widows, even those who did not marry again, could fulfill the norms set down by St. Paul for acceptance among the special group that constituted the "widowhood" in the technical sense. There must have been a number of younger widows of good reputation at least in the larger communities. Undoubtedly as long as they did not marry again, they were placed on the lists of the wards of the Christian community and given special privileges, as well as the right to become objects of its special charitable concern. The very fact that certain conditions seemed to have been set down for admission into the "widowhood" has led some scholars to identify the term "widow" used in this technical sense with "deaconess."

That there were widows in certain Christian communities who in fact were not deaconesses is clear, for instance, from the *Apostolic Constitutions*. This source clearly indicates that widows must obey "bishops, priests, deacons and deaconesses." On the other hand, the *Testament of Our Lord,* obviously making use of the term "widow" in the technical sense, places the ones who have received the "blessing proper to their state from a bishop" over the order of deaconesses, warning them to watch over the female deacons. This document also presents an interesting order for the reception of Communion according to rank. Widows are to receive immediately after the male deacons, while the deaconesses could approach the table after the children but before the married adults.

Perhaps some plausible explanation can be offered for this confusing use of terms. In earliest times deaconesses may well have been chosen in accordance with the norms that St. Paul set down for the "widowhood." They all indeed had to be widows, married only once, at least sixty years old, honorable, hospitable, charitable, enjoying a good reputation in the community. Evidence for this opinion is found in an edict of Theodosius issued in 390. This document repeats word for word the substance of the Apostle's command. But it substitutes the word "deaconess" where the Apostle used the term "widow." But certainly by 390, and perhaps even by the beginning of the second century if we have interpreted correctly the statement of St. Ignatius of Antioch which we presented above, St. Paul's norms represented not a law or precept, but an ideal. The Church had grown tremendously. It boasted of a vast female membership. Great numbers of women had to be baptized and instructed. There were large numbers at the assemblies, and undoubtedly many who could not always attend because they were sick or poor. To minister to these women a large staff of deaconesses would have been required in the more populous areas. Yet there simply could not have been enough widows available in all the communities who met with all of Paul's requirements. Nor, perhaps, were women of sixty and older able to do all that the ministry in those times of gigantic expansion required of them. So the practical exigencies of the period might well have forced admission into the order of deaconesses of younger widows and even virgins. But since from earliest times the practice was to employ in this ministry qualified widows, the terms "widow" and "widowhood" were still used in some documents of a

later period as a technical term in referring to the deaconesses
of these times whether they actually were widows or not. But
of course the terms do not always have to be used in this
technical sense. Sometimes they are employed to refer to
women who are really widows, whether deaconesses or not.
And herein lies a source of confusion.

Possibly because the apostolic injunction required for admission into the widowhood not only abstinence from a second marriage but also positive evidence of a life of chastity,
celibacy seems to have become one of the first requirements in
later times for the order of deaconesses. As time went on
there were evidences that the celibate state of these women
had to be confirmed by vow. Violation of such a vow was
punished by excommunication on the part of the Church, as
well as, in certain instances, by severe penalties on the part of
the state. In the Empire any person found guilty of seducing a
deaconess was to be put to death by the sword.

We have already indicated that since deaconesses were in
later times employed as teachers of catechism one of the pre-
requisites for admission into the order was the acquisition of
some basic theological knowledge. This did not seem to have
been imparted in formal schools, as so often it was in the case
of the male clergy, but through a kind of private tutoring during a period of apprenticeship and probation.

There seems to be no evidence that in the earliest times the
deaconesses were in any way bound by a promise or vow of
poverty. Later on, however, laws forbidding ownership of
property to them began to appear. In the early days apparently many lived with their close relatives and enjoyed whatever of this world's goods their family could supply. Later
regulations, however, required them to live in quasi-monastic
institutions and imposed on them restrictions with regard to
the disposition of their property. There is some indication that
during this period they were able to make use personally of

the fruits of the benefices that were established to support them.

The confusion encountered in trying to relate widowhood with the order of deaconess is further compounded when we come to consider the use of the words *episcopa* and *presbytera* (bishopess and priestess). Did widowhood ever imply enlistment in an order higher than that of deaconess? We have already mentioned the use of the term "bishopess" in two funeral inscriptions. E. Diehl in his collection of ancient Latin Christian inscriptions cites a good example of an epitaph from Tropaea in Calabria commemorating the death of a certain Leta, a priestess (*presbytera*). It is unlikely that a young woman would be called *presbytera* unless that word were used, just as the word *vidua* came to be, in a technical sense. Analysts have recognized this fact. But some have opined that the words *episcopa* and *presbytera* are technical terms applied in the early Christian community to the wives of bishops and priests. There is, though, a definite difficulty with this solution. Very often in funeral inscriptions—in fact, almost invariably if the husband is a man of some rank—mention is made of the husband on his wife's epitaph. Archaeology records thousands of examples of this practice in early Christian burial. Those who would claim that the terms *episcopa* and *presbytera* refer to the wives of bishops and priests have offered no explanation of why the names of their prominent husbands are singularly missing from these funeral inscriptions.

There are examples in the writings of the Fathers in which these terms clearly refer to the wives of ecclesiastics. Undoubtedly a case in point is found in the *Dialogues* of St. Gregory the Great. He mentions a certain priest by the name of Stephen, who from the time of his priestly ordination, kept his "priestess" (*presbyteram suam*) at a distance, loving her as a sister, but also fearing her as a possible threat to his chastity. Canon 21 of the Council of Auxerre (c. 570–90)

states that it is unlawful for a priest after he has received
his blessing to sleep in the same bed with his "priestess" or
to indulge his flesh.

On the other hand, there are a number of texts which
would be difficult to understand if the terms *episcopa* and
presbytera signified only the wives of bishops and priests. In
one of his letters St. Gregory the Great mentions an abbess
who refused to wear the monastic garb, but lived all her life in
the vestments which the priestesses (*presbyterae*) of her area
were wont to wear. But there is no evidence that any special
kind of garb was prescribed for the wives of priests, nor that
they customarily wore any particular kind of dress. Canon 11
of the Council of Laodicea speaks of priestesses (*preby-
tidas*) or presidents of the assembly. Isidore Mercator, commentator on the text, tells us that here the Council is referring
to those women who in the Latin Church are called widows,
ones who have married only once, are of advanced age, and
have been entrusted with a position of responsibility in the
community. These, he says, the Greeks call "priestesses" (*presbyterae*). St. Epiphanius in his *Adversus Haereses* expresses
his dissatisfaction with the term *presbytidae*. Women ministers should not be given that appellation, lest anyone mis-
takenly attribute to them the sacerdotal dignity. They do not
have true priestly power; they do not have the right of offering
sacrifice to God. He would lead us to believe that here again
we have another term that the early Church applied to the order of deaconesses.

Perhaps we can offer some solution for this additional dilemma of terminology by applying to it the same argument
we used with the word "widow." Originally in accordance
with the injunction of St. Paul only elderly widows were admitted into the order of deaconesses. Later on when there was
a greater demand for women ministers, the Apostle's specifica-
tions were not taken literally. Not only elderly widows, but
younger ones as well as virgins were admitted into the ranks

of the deaconesses. But just as the word "widow" in these later times might have been applied to a deaconess whether she was in fact one or not, so also, perhaps, the Greek term "elder": *presbytera,* priestess. What in early times signified a canonical requirement was in later eras retained as a technical term. This might be as true for the words *presbytera* or *presbytida* as it is for the word *vidua.*

Perhaps a similar explanation can be offered for the word *episcopa.* In the early Church all the clergy seemed to have places in the choir. The chief liturgist's place was the highest so that he could supervise or oversee the whole proceedings. So he was called the *episkopos,* the overseer. The presbyteral college sat around him. The deacons performed their respective ministerial tasks in various parts of the assembly. The deaconesses were assigned to special seats in the area reserved for women. They sat in a prominent place in this section, just as the bishop did in the whole assembly, so that they could look over the group of women and lead them in worship. This could very well be what the Council of Laodicea was referring to when it called them presidents of the assembly. So it is easy to see how the term *episcopai* (overseers) might occasionally be applied to them.

The ancient documents which mention deaconesses acknowledge their having a place among the hierarchy of ecclesiastics. But as has already been intimated there is no complete consensus as to their exact rank in the structure. All agree in placing them under bishops, priests and deacons. It also seems clear that they outranked clerics in minor orders, with the exception, perhaps, of lectors. Their relationship to the subdeacons is close, for some sources seem to place them on a par with clerics of this rank. They are reminded that their chief duty is to assist the deacons. They are warned against usurping the prerogatives of the priests and deacons. They are constantly reminded that their ministry is limited to the performance of diaconal tasks for the women members of the congregation. Some documents refer to them as porters, or doorkeepers, of the women's assembly. The *Apostolic Constitutions* infer that even a deacon could excommunicate them for a breach of discipline. But the same document secures their right to a decent sustenance by law in the same way it provides for the rest of the clergy. Of the offerings and gifts presented by the faithful at the Eucharist a suitable selection is made for the oblation of the sacrifice. But what remains over and above is to be divided among the clergy as follows: bishops were to have four parts, priests three, deacons two, and subdeacons, lectors, singers and deaconesses one. Various legal codes also rank them among the clergy, so that, like other members of the priestly entourage, they could be punished for certain categories of crimes for which the laity received either no or at least less severe penalties.

The later centuries witnessed a decline in the order. As we said, in the earliest times the principal and most useful function of the deaconesses was to assist in the baptism of adult women converts. As the Church grew and whole nations became Christian, infant baptism became the rule, and fewer and fewer adults received the sacrament. So certain communities felt less of a need for the ministrations of the order. From the sixth century on in the Western Church deaconesses were on the wane. There are few indications that they continued to be used in the baptismal ritual. They busied themselves more with various kinds of charitable enterprises. Though their role in baptism was for all practical purposes lost, they tried to assume greater responsibilities in the Eucharistic celebrations. The legislation emanating from synods and councils of the period is rife with warnings against encroachment upon the prerogatives of the male clergy at the altar. Later on in the history of the Church there is evidence of a growing friction between the order of deaconesses and a proliferating female monastic population. In the Middle Ages abbesses of certain communities were wont to receive ordination as deaconesses so as not to seem to their religious subjects less important in the service of the Lord than the ordained women who served in the diaconate. Gradually the focus of activity for deaconesses shifted from the baptistry, sanctuary and classroom to the monastery. The acceptance of religious life eventually became for all practical purposes a necessary condition for ordination. Even from the fifth century there are evidences of the existence of monasteries open to religious of both sexes, some of which were under the presidency of an abbess. Mervyn Archdall has reproduced in his *Monasticon hibernicum* the chronicle of a mixed abbey in County Kildare, Ireland. Allegedly, it was founded in 484 by St. Bridget, and the chronicler notes that during her lifetime Bridget presided over the whole community, men and women alike. Later on in history there are accounts of abbesses, seated on thrones and equipped with miter and crosier, presiding over their mixed community while one of the priests offered Mass.

As early as the sixth century certain local and provincial councils began to prohibit entirely the ordination of women. The Council of Orleans (533), for instance, betrays a growing spirit of male chauvinism: henceforth no woman is to be given the responsibilities ensuing from ordination to the diaconate because women are simply too fickle to manage them well. To be sure, this anti-feminine bias was not something new in the Church. An examination of the works of many of the early Fathers of the Church betrays that these men, who for so many centuries subsequently exercised such an influence on the tradition of the Church, were quite suspicious of ordained women and decidedly unsympathetic with women in general. Their constantly repeated warnings and reservations about deaconesses began in the period just preceding the Dark Ages to take their toll in the legislation that eventually was to abound in almost every quarter of the Church. Typical was the attitude of St. Epiphanius, who constantly harped upon the theme that deaconesses were never to do anything

more than well-established tradition would allow. He seems to
be at his eloquent best when he chides those who would in
their behavior give the slightest impression that they were
usurping truly priestly functions in the Church. He argues
that if any woman would have been worthy to be a priest, it
was Mary, the Mother of Jesus. But she was not even given
the right to baptize. Deaconesses are tolerated for one reason
alone: to preserve the modesty of the male clergy in the baptismal liturgy and other functions. Other Fathers write in a
similar vein, and the prestige of these men had eventually to
doom the order of deaconesses to extinction when the primary
reason for their existence disappeared. But the order did
not die as easily in the East as it did in the West. There are evidences of ordinations in the East as late as the thirteenth century, and in churches separated from Rome even much later,
as we shall see. But just as in the West, the later decline of
the order in the East seems to have been preceded by a flight
from the market place to the monasteries.

The theological tradition which has been most influential
in our times. was one that was formed from the thirteenth
down through the eighteenth century. This tradition never
denied the existence of deaconesses in the early Church. It
acknowledged that these women assisted with baptisms, had a
role to play in the liturgical assemblies, and enjoyed considerable prestige in the community because of their charitable enterprises. What it did was much worse for the theologian and
historian considering the question today. Admitting all the
data connected with the operation of the deaconesses in pris-
tine times, it denied that these women were truly ordained.

St. Thomas was one of the principal authors of this tradition. In the *Supplement* to the *Summa* (q. 39, a. 1) he asks
whether a woman can be ordained. He answers that from the
very nature of the sacrament of orders itself—and hence not
merely from any positive legislation on the part of the
Church—any attempt to ordain a woman would be invalid.

The reason is that the sacrament of orders essentially implies an elevation, a promotion to a position of prominence in the Christian community. But woman has been placed by God himself in a state of subjection, of submission. Therefore it is impossible for a woman to be ordained. No doubt the minor premise of the Angelic Doctor's argument has to do with an interpretation of Scripture and a view of original sin that would not be upheld in all theological quarters today.

St. Thomas views deaconesses in the early Church as participants only in the functions proper to deacons, not in their ordained, hierarchial status. He had in mind, it would seem, a situation similar to one which exists today. A laywoman can under certain conditions distribute Communion. This traditionally is a diaconal function; that is, it is one proper to only ordained priests and deacons in the Church. But because of circumstances, the dearth of priests and deacons, the supreme authority in the Church has given permission for lay people to perform this function. But they do it not in virtue of ordination which would make them official ministers of the Church, but in virtue of the special permission given them by ecclesiastical authority to engage in this diaconal function. Thus without actually being ordained a person can participate legitimately in acts proper to a recognized order. So it was with the deaconesses in the early Church.

Needless to say, up to very recent times practically all Catholic theologians have followed St. Thomas' opinion in this matter, whether for the same reason or not. They admit some historical evidence for a ceremony of ordination similar to that of the male deacons. But on *a priori* grounds they deny that such an ordination is sacramental. Women are not apt subjects for sacramental ordination. Therefore these ceremonies could not have been real ordinations. It is, of course, difficult to refute such an argument. To challenge it on *a priori* grounds would be to fall into the same trap and be open to the same accusation of prejudice. The only true solution is the one that is substantiated by historical evidence. But since sacramentality was never an issue for the early Church, it cannot be proven that these ordinations were considered sacramental ones. As a matter of fact, when early documents treat of the ordination of male deacons, they do not mention grace or the sacramental character. There is really no historical evidence that male deacons were sacramentally ordained either. The sources use the very same expressions of female ordinations as they do of male ones. In regard to the deaconesses they speak of an imposition of hands, of ordination, of receiving the blessing, of being listed among the clergy, or in the catalogue of priests, etc. To push any historical argument against the sacramentality of the ordination of deaconesses too far would result also in a necessary denial of the sacramentality of the ordination of male deacons. Yet despite the lack of so many words in a historical document to prove it, traditional theology has always recognized the validity and sacramentality of the ordination of male deacons.

An argument against the ordination of deaconesses is lodged in the fact that some early documents deny them the power of dispensing the sacraments, of sanctifying or blessing. Thus the *Apostolic Constitutions* state: "A deaconess does not bless or perform any work belonging to the office of presbyters or deacons. . . ." But the same section of the document denies this power to the deacons also: "A deacon does not bless; he does not give the benediction; rather he receives it from the bishop and priest; he does not baptize; he does not offer; but when a bishop or priest has offered, he distributes to the people, not as a priest, but as one who ministers to the priests. . . ." The idea of the character of the diaconate as a sacramental power to sanctify does not seem to have been fully developed in the early Church. The power to sanctify is accorded to neither male nor female deacon, but to bishops and priests alone.

Since there is a definite parallelism in the way the sources treat both the male and female deacons, it would seem inequitable to say that the males were really ordained while the females were not. From a consideration of functions and prerogatives alone the unprejudiced scholar has no more reason to say that the males had real power to bless emanating from their sacramental ordination than to say the exact opposite: that is, that the females had such power while the males did not. To present an effective argument against the ordained status of the deaconesses, a theologian would have to adduce texts asserting that hands were to be imposed only upon the male deacons, not upon the deaconesses. He could do it, because there are prohibitions in certain quarters against laying hands on deaconesses. But on the other hand, there are certain texts that indicate that they are ordained through an imposition of hands! The only solution to the dilemma seems to stem from the possibility that in the early Church different views could have prevailed in different places at different times.

The fifteenth canon of the Council of Chalcedon indicates quite clearly that deaconesses receive ordination from the bishop through a laying on of hands. Both of the technical terms that customarily describe this action as true ordination are used (*xeirotonia* and *xeirothesia*). The Council also describes the ministry of these women which results from their ordination as a *leitourgia*.

Another interesting indication is presented in the *Apostolic Constitutions* where the Apostle Bartholomew is depicted as making provision for the ordination of deaconesses: "Concerning a deaconess, I, Bartholomew, make this regulation: Bishop, you will lay hands upon her in the presence of the assembly of priests and of deacons and of deaconesses; and you will say: 'Eternal God, the Father of our Lord Jesus Christ, the creator of man and woman, you filled Miriam, Deborah, Anna and Hulda with your Spirit; you deemed it proper that your Only-Begotten should be born of a woman; in the tabernacle of the Old Law as well as in the Temple you ordained that women should be the gate-keepers. Look down now upon this, your handmaid, who is to be ordained to the office of deaconess. Give her your Holy Spirit. Cleanse from her all sordidness of flesh and spirit, so that she may worthily discharge the duty that is committed to her for your glory and for the praise of your Christ; to him be adoration and praise, as well as to you and the Holy Spirit forever. Amen.'"

The *Apostolic Constitutions* emanate from late fourth-century Syria. The *Apostolic Tradition* of Hippolytus, on the other hand, represents a Roman tradition two centuries earlier. It is argued by some theologians that this latter document, representing an earlier and more authentic tradition, expressly forbids the laying on of hands in the case of deaconesses.

But the *Apostolic Tradition* does not use the word "deaconess" at all. The pertinent passage refers to widows, and brings us back to the problem of the relationship of deaconesses to widows again. The text states that a widow is chosen, but not ordained (*ou xeirotoneitai*). She is tested for some time after the death of her husband. Then if found without fault she may be placed upon the community's roster of widows. Again it is stated that she is not ordained, because she does not offer sacrifice and has nothing to do with liturgical services. She is assigned only to pray on behalf of the community. A later passage, however, refers to a special meal (perhaps an *agapē*) that is celebrated in honor of widows in the late afternoon. A possible reference is made here to the clerical status of widows, but the text is not clear enough to give a certain reading.

In considering the relationship between widows and deaconesses in very early times, we have already stated that a distinction was made between the two. Some deaconesses were widows; others were not, and there were widows who were not deaconesses. In other words, it is not to be presumed in rather early documents that the word "widow" is used in its later technical sense to refer to a deaconess, whether she be a widow or not. Hippolytus may well have been concerned about reports which, perhaps, he heard from other communities where the practice of ordaining widows was already in vogue. His seems to be a call back to the strict interpretation and reading of the text of First Timothy where there is no mention of ordination of widows. At any rate, it does not seem licit to interpret the word "widow" in this early document in the technical sense in which it was used in later documents to refer to deaconesses. The process of identification of the widowhood with the order of deaconesses could not have been completed in all areas by this early date.

A second objection can be drawn from the eleventh canon of the Council of Laodicea held in the middle of the fourth century. It states: "It is not proper to ordain priestesses or presidents of the assembly."

By the time this canon was formulated, of course, the technical language was well developed, and as we have said, the word "priestess" here very likely refers to the deaconesses. The theologians who propose this objection presume that what the Council forbade was the ordination of deaconesses as such. Deaconesses could be employed, but they were not to be ordained. However, it does not seem, even from the very text of the canon, that ordination was the abuse that the Council had a mind to correct. It would seem that the qualification "or presidents of the assembly" receives a certain emphasis in explaining what the "priestesses" were doing. We saw that the principal reason for the existence of the order of deaconesses in the very earliest times was to minister baptism to women. By now this reason could not be used. What the Council states is that presidency over the assembly is not a sufficient reason to ordain deaconesses: they should not be ordained for this task. Moreover, the text of the canon does not seem to imply that if they were ordained only for this purpose, such an ordination would be invalid. The words in which the directive is couched do not imply an absolute prohibition, but only an opinion about the propriety or impropriety of such an action. But whatever may be the meaning of this canon, the fact is that a century later the Council of Chalcedon would speak approvingly of the ordination of deaconesses to fulfill the ministry for which the Church needed them.

A third objection is taken from the nineteenth canon of the Council of Nicaea. The canon requires that converts from the Paulician heresy be baptized again in the Catholic Church. After their conversion and baptism in the Church those who had been clerics in the sect might be ordained by a Catholic bishop. But if they have been unworthy of the office to which they had been assigned they are to be deposed. Deaconesses are to be treated in the same way. But the Council warns that those deaconesses in the sect who had not received ordination through an imposition of hands, when they are received into the Church, are to be considered as being no different from laywomen.

The first part of the canon relating to deaconesses presumes the existence in the Paulician sect of at least some who had been ordained through an imposition of hands. These were, seemingly, to be processed like other clergy converted from heresy: they were to be baptized again, tested and eventually ordained by a Catholic bishop if they proved worthy. The second part of the canon cautions that there were in the sect some deaconesses that were not ordained. They were not to be ordained when received in the Catholic Church either, but treated as laywomen.

Actually this canon offers as much of an argument for as it does against the practice of ordaining deaconesses in the early Church. It simply gives indication that there were in the Paulician sect two classes of deaconesses, one ordained for service in the assembly and in sacramental ministry, the other

not ordained but dedicated to the performance of certain
charitable works in the community. Some researchers believe
that the same division prevailed in the Catholic Church at certain times and places. They would contend that this was the
case not only for deaconesses but for male deacons as well.

The final problem that we shall consider is one that originated as late as 1736 in the renowned synod of the Maronite
Church held on Mount Lebanon. The Maronites are a group
of Eastern rite Catholics united to Rome. The acts of this
synod were approved by the Holy See. Apropos of deaconesses, the synod made the following provisions. They had to
be chosen from among vowed virgins, or widows who had
been married only once and vowed perpetual chastity upon
their entry into the diaconate. They legitimately assumed diaconal chores when they were consecrated in the order by an
episcopal blessing. Among these chores were the guarding of
the doors of the women's section of the churches, the ushering
of women to their proper place in the assembly, to assist
women about to be baptized in managing their clothing and
to help in the actual baptism, to apply oil to the bodies of
women in the administration of the sacraments of baptism,
confirmation and the anointing of the sick. It was also their
task to wash and prepare the bodies of deceased women for
burial. One of their most important roles was to explain the
truths of the faith to women converts as well as to Christian
women who had been poorly instructed. They were the in-
termediates between the male clergy and women faithful in
any public negotiations. They were authorized to give character references to the responsible persons for women of their
community seeking jobs with the Church. They were enlisted
by the ecclesiastical authorities to help in reported cases of violation of consecrated virgins. They were also to act as admin-
istrators of the properties of cloistered female religious.

The synod readily admitted that for a long time there had
been no need to have deaconesses assist in the administration

of the sacraments. Adult baptisms were a rarity; the whole
body was no longer anointed in any of the sacraments. But it
did seem good to the bishops assembled at the synod to seek
the approval of the Holy See in promoting abbesses of the rite
to the order of deaconesses to expedite certain problems that
had arisen among female religious. The abbesses were to have
all of the rights and privileges that the order of deaconesses
had enjoyed from time immemorial, even though they might
not find occasion to exercise all of them. It was made clear,
however, that they were not to function at the altar, or even
give Communion to their subjects when no priest or deacon
was available. The synod left bishops of the rite free to ordain
or not, as they saw fit, abbesses within their jurisdiction to the
diaconate. But they could do so only for an urgent reason after having assured themselves of both the complete orthodoxy
of the doctrine and inviolability of the chastiy of the candidates.

By the time this decree was promulgated, of course, the
ideas of the medieval theologians and canonists had thoroughly permeated the Western Church. One would not have
expected the Holy See to approve of these arrangements, but it
did. The intent of the Maronite bishops at the synod obviously
was only to reinstate in certain female monasteries in some
modified sense the order of deaconesses that had flourished in
the rite in ancient times. Perhaps the reason that the acts of
the synod were approved without emendation was that they
remain quite ambiguous on the issue of ordination. One section employs the word "ordain" (*ordinare*) in relation to the
deaconesses. Another sees them dedicated to their tasks
through an episcopal blessing, presumably, much after the
fashion of abbesses in the Western Church. A third section
declares rather blatantly that only a male is capable of being
ordained. Thus the significance of this synod relative to the
question of ordained women cannot be great, for it can assure
us only of the existence of a group of women empowered to

perform some few diaconal tasks and entitled to call themselves deaconesses in the Maronite Church of this period with the approval of the Holy See. At least as far as Rome was concerned, obviously, no case whatsoever could be made for their sacramental ordination.

Woman's lot has hardly been a happy one in the Church. She has alternately received highest praise and foulest vituperation. But generally in the eyes of ecclesiastics the Eve in her has prevailed over the Mary. Tertullian and St. Jerome call her the gateway to hell. The famous inquisitor Cardinal Juan de Torquemada sees her nature as inferior, easily corruptible and prone to lying. The renowned canonist Henry of Segusio sees her only salvation in a completely servile subjection to men to the extent that a wife on a day of strict fast and abstinence would believe it a greater sin to disobey the directive of her husband demanding that she serve meat than the law of the Church. What is amazing is that even in the face of such blind and un-Christian prejudice she was still accorded some kind of ministerial role in the community. History bears certain witness at least to that. But in addition there seems to be evidence of a tradition about that ministry that was broad enough to support a number of different customs, practices and understandings. As was said, it seems that the issue of whether there should be women ministers or not in our time cannot and should not be settled on the basis of tradition alone. The question today has to be decided on the issue which emerges in tradition as the one dominant factor: whether such a ministry is meaningful and serves some necessary or highly useful objective in the apostolate of the Church in the world at this time in history. If that question has to be answered in the affirmative, then there should be no obstacle placed to the establishment of a distaff priesthood on the part of a Church that has always believed and professed, but even more so today, that God placed the salvation of the whole world in the hands of a woman.

CHAPTER IV

The Priest as a Man of Faith

The problem of priests' abandonment of their ministerial role today certainly admits of no simple solution. The motives underlying such behavior are obviously highly complex. No priest cavalierly leaves that to which he has dedicated himself by a deeply spiritual and intense academic commitment. Surveys have indicated that lack of job satisfaction, difficulties with the way authority is exercised in certain quarters of the Church and problems with the law of celibacy top the list of reasons why priests turn to other occupations. Most priests who leave the ministry remain active Catholics. But there are some who are prompted to leave the priesthood by a loss of faith. To be sure, many of the older priests who go feel that the Catholic faith itself has substantially changed, and that now they are forced to become involved in something that they did not bargain for and were not able to foresee when they were in the seminary. Many priests who remain in active service also feel that the clergy are divided on fundamentals, that there really is no unanimity of belief among priests, and this is a cause of distress to them. The cohesiveness of the clergy in times past was one of the chief factors promoting an excellent *esprit* and one of the best sources of support amid the vexing difficulties of priestly life. Now not many priests feel that unifying power of faith. It is only natural to ask why.

Modern theology has not attempted to redefine faith. It is still seen as an assent to what has been revealed by God precisely because it is God who is the revealer. But there is a shift of emphasis from what scholastic theologians would call the material object to the formal object or motive of faith. Whereas yesterday's theology stressed what was revealed, today's concentrates on the revealer. Faith is considered primarily as a commitment to the One who is all-knowing and all-truthful. Really it is only because of this prior personal commitment that one can assent to what God says.

There is hardly a priest who at some time or another has not felt that, no matter how one tries to present it, certain religious matters seem quite irrelevant in today's world. Yet at times one can perceive what seems to be a stir of excitement, an air of expectancy, in the Church. Christians seem to be waiting for some miracle to happen that will restore the faith of New Testament times. Some people seem to be hoping for a new appearance of God in the world today. Then they will believe; or at least then they will feel that their faith has been vindicated. But is it really true that faith springs from miracles? Do not, instead, miracles spring from faith, as the New Testament so often indicates? The hard fact that others in the Church are coming more and more to realize is that faith demands God's hiddenness just as much, if not more, than it demands his self-disclosure. Faith has to be founded on God's absence as well as on his presence. And it is this ambivalence that seems to have divided believers today into two camps.

One group sees faithfulness today requiring the banishment of God from the world, the secularization of society, and the promulgation of the notion that, as far as true believers are concerned, God must be considered dead. For these the meaning of the incarnation, and in particular that aspect of the incarnation which Pauline theology terms the kenosis (the concealment of the glory accruing to the Word in virtue of his divinity by his human guise), is that true faith in God demands that man face up to the responsibilities God has entrusted to him. It is cheap faith just to believe in God. It is genuine faith to believe in the fact that God has placed the management of this world and concomitant accountability for it entirely in the hands of men, to believe that God wants man to live without him, without the reassurance of his divinity to fall back on. It is God's faith in man that is really the central fact of all revelaton. The Church's liturgy constantly reminds believers of this, for its central symbolism reveals them as identified with Christ in his mystical body, as one with him in Communion, as doing the "thing" of Christ in acting out his paschal and pentecostal mystery. God trusts his faithful to continue the work of Christ in the world today. He is confident that they will not misuse their freedom to reject the promptings of the Spirit; this is what the Good News proclaims. Yet man cannot really accept this fact. He prefers just to believe in God. He knows himself too well. He cannot have faith in himself, and so he cannot believe that God has faith in him. So to those who accept this perspective on faith, the Christian today has become as faithless as the Jew of old reprimanded in the New Testament texts. He has not really accepted God's word. He cannot believe in God as he really is. He has fashioned for himself a god according to his own ideas. He has made God just another idol. In the name of faith he has committed the ultimate sin of unfaithfulness. He has deified himself and his own notions. He cannot abide by the teaching of Bonhoeffer that the God who is really with us is the God that has abandoned us.

The other group of believers views faithfulness as adherence to the traditional interpretation of God's revelation: to that primordial revelation of God to Moses when he styled himself as Yahweh, the one who is ever present. The true believer is the one who in his life witnesses the presence of God, not his absence. He lives in such a way that, if there were no God, his life would have no meaning. His life itself is the miracle that springs from faith and is at the very time the foundation of that faith. Without God his life would be absurd. He is not ashamed of the fact that he really needs God. Only God can relieve his existential *Angst;* only God can put meaning into his existence. He is honest with himself. He tries to be humble. He knows that to banish God from his life leaves no alternative but to apotheosize himself. To believe that God has such faith in man as to withdraw from his life, to play dead as far as man is concerned, is to force man to put his faith ultimately not in God but in himself. This for him is the unredeemable crime of pride and idolatry. He would rather see God as a projection rooted in his own needs than to destroy himself in the narcissistic pool of his own arrogance.

To be a priest in the world today means to live at the very vortex of this dialectic. It means to have an ultimate concern and personal orientation that is, and perhaps must be, in the ultimate analysis ambivalent. It may imply having an identity, a role in the world, that is basically schizoid. It may well be that because of this confusion, because of this uncertainty, because of this double view of faith, it is easier to be a Christian today than it was in the past. But it is harder to be a priest. For a priest is cast by others in a role of responsibility and leadership. And he may well seem to himself to be presiding over chaos. And if today it is difficult to be a priest, it is much more difficult to be a priest who is a genuine person.

The priest of the past felt that his priesthood was rooted in the celebration of Christ's paschal mystery. He was the official representative of the whole people of God in the re-enactment of this mystery at the altar. His role could be perceived as a truly prophetic one. The Church was apprehended by the faithful as the very body of Christ on the current scene. It fully commanded the priest's loyalty for he looked upon it as the source of the continuing revelation by God of himself in

Christ for peoples of all times and all places. The priest as a minister of that body uttered a word that was interpreted as God's own. Inasmuch as his life too reflected that word which he proclaimed, the priest himself was considered, as much as anyone can be, to be truly another Christ. This was his dignity. In this reflection he found his mission in life.

But in today's divided world some priests are of the opinion that all this has changed. They see the priest as the witness not of the Parousia, the presence of God and his Christ, but of the kenosis, the perceived absence of the divine. Can there be any real celebration or any meaningful prophecy in a world stripped of an awareness of the presence of God? Can there be authentic prayer in such a world? Does not existence itself have to be a kind of prayer—indeed the only one that can have significance when God is understood as having freely sought to be other to himself in the kenosis? And is not existence itself a call to man to imitate God, to stand out from himself, to be other to himself, to risk himself, his very being and personhood, to sacrifice life itself in what appears in the final logical analysis to be totally absurd? If God in some sense died to himself, if he mortified himself in the kenosis, if he ceased to prize what man from the beginning has always desired, his Godhead, his immortality, when he freely chose to be other to himself, to become man, then this was the absurdity of all absurdities.

So some say that the priest today is not called to be a witness of the paschal mystery, much less to celebrate it. His task is a much more difficult and fearsome one. If God is, in the words of the Orestean theologians, the failure of man, then the priest has to be the failure of God. His calling might well be to be a failure. He cannot dedicate himself just to act out or celebrate the paschal mystery. That would be meaningless in a world that still cannot appreciate it and in so many ways evidences its rejection of it. As the unique, irreplaceable, responsible and totally human person that he is, the priest today is called upon to live the paschal mystery. And he must live it in its stark reality and absurdity—on Calvary, not in the magnificence of the temple; in nakedness, not in the caparison of high ritualism; in the ambivalence of suspension between heaven and earth, not in the reassuring solidity of a marble pulpit or oaken professorial chair; in the useless and wasteful spilling out of his life, not in the comfort and security of a meaningful existence. He must live it today without prop or mask. He cannot resort to priestcraft. He cannot find comfort in shiny chalice, blanched host or soul-stirring song. He cannot distract himself from its opprobrium by shamanism. As priest he can boast of no special personal powers. He cannot use evil eye or magnetic personality. He is not a counselor or community builder. He is not a humanitarian or philanthropist. His life must forever proclaim that God is not what man would be if man were God. Rather man is what God chose to be when he decided not to appear as God. The priest today is called upon to be and to do what perhaps he did not bargain for. He has to have the courage to come face to face in his very life with the *tremendum* and *fascinosum* of the paschal mystery. And in fear and trembling he must pronounce over his own being the awesome words of its consecration: "My God, my God, why have you forsaken me?"

But his deep and living faith will tell such a priest that what he is living is really the paschal mystery, and the paschal mystery does not end in death and defeat; rather it is basically a message of hope to those who have the courage to accept their humanity. For through death it leads to resurrection, through absurdity to real meaning, through risk to security, through ignominy to glory.

The current crisis of faith assumes even more imposing proportions when a priest considers that it is necessary for him to believe not only in God and his own humanity, but also in the Church. Here at times there seems to be an almost impossible credibility gap. For the Church does not seem at times to believe in or act upon its own doctrine. It appears to disbelieve its own power to believe. It often responds to challenges not at all like a credal community inspired by love, but after the fashion of a worldly organization, a state, with laws and punishments. It refuses to take the risk of trusting that the doctrine it received from Christ will really be understood by men or will be able to inspire them. It speaks of the Spirit, but seems at times to put more reliance on purely human devices and ploys. It can live comfortably only with the self-concept of statehood suggested to it by the territorial donations of Pepin and Charlemagne. It feeds on its history and tradition more than on its doctrine. The Council of Trent, for example, under the guidance of the Spirit, defined against Luther the orthodox doctrine that human nature is basically good and not totally corrupted. But then the very same Council seemed to give the lie to its own pronouncement by multiplying laws, regulations and punishments. Arnold Toynbee has remarked that the whole course of world events today might have been completely altered if the Roman Curia in the seventeenth century had acted upon its own doctrine. Red China might not have emerged, and India might well have been a completely Christian nation. The Church has always believed that salvation is for all men, that the Gospel message is of universal appeal. It has always maintained that its doctrine is not eternally wedded to any one particular philosophical system or to the Western way of life. Yet when pioneer missionaries like Matteo Ricci and Roberto de' Nobili tried to adapt the teaching of the Church to the philosophy and life-style of the peoples of China and India in the seventeenth century, the gigantic strides they took in making converts, despite the fact that their methods received approval from several popes, were ultimately nullified by the decrees of the Congregation of Propaganda. All future missionaries to these countries were required to take an oath that they would not indulge in so-called "Oriental rites." It was only in 1939 that these decrees were revoked in regard to China. But by then it was too late.

So it is that some theologians of our time have pointed a finger of accusation at the Church. Is it really dedicated to the Gospel doctrine of love and concern for people? Is the tactic that a priest must employ to manifest genuine pastoral regard for his people one of rebellion against the myriad rules and regulations that have issued forth from ecclesiastical authorities? Must he be constantly torn apart because of his love for the Church and his love for people, when he believes in the depths of his heart the doctrine articulated in Vatican II that people really are the Church?

No light can be shed on the problem by introducing, as some theologians of our time might be suspected of having done, a distinction between the official and charismatic Church. This would strike at the very root of the theory of priesthood that we have proposed. There is in reality and can be only one Church. And in that Church there is as a matter of fact and by divine intention a magisterial authority, specially assisted by the Spirit when it performs its proper task, if not when it acts like a state or other secular institution. This has from time immemorial been the belief of orthodox faith.

But there is an older distinction that might be of some use to theology today. Paschase Radbert, for instance, wrote in the ninth century: "One cannot say, properly speaking: 'I believe in my neighbor, or in an angel, or in any creature whatsoever.' Throughout Holy Scripture you will find the correct use of this profession of faith reserved for God alone. . . . Therefore do not say: 'I believe in the holy Catholic Church,' but, 'I believe the holy Catholic Church.'" Now we do and must say that we believe *in* the holy Catholic Church inasmuch as it is a divine institution: that is, we believe that its roots, basic structure and certain of its prerogatives are divine. But the distinction may still be valid if it is applied to the Church existentially, for it is also a formally human insti-

tution; that is, it is composed of men, and indeed of men who
are sinners; and so, though basically authentic and good, as
are the men who make it up, the Church is also capable of error, of evil and of inconsistency. Though its faith, guided by
God, will reject Pelagianism, its life may well reflect it. Faith
in God, reflecting man's ultimate concern, demands total self-
commitment. This kind of faith has to be reserved for God
alone. Faith in the Church, on the other hand, demands acceptance of it as the means God has established through Christ
to lead men to himself. While such faith is certainly concerned with ultimates, it is not in itself an expression of ultimate concern. Indeed it is only in the light of some such distinction as this that we can interpret the actions of some of
the Church's leading protagonists as evidencing faith and
not disbelief. Take, for instance, St. Catherine of Siena, who
railed fearlessly against the policies of some of the popes,
confronting them, and warning them; or Peter the Chanter,
who warned that the word of God even in the Church could
be made void because of the traditions of men.

There is reason to believe that even in our theologically
sophisticated era we have not been able to conquer a most
pernicious ecclesiological error which seems constantly to
plague the Church: a false idealism which cannot accept the
human element in the Church. Idealists, whether heretical
like the Manichaeans, Cathars and Jansenists or perfectly orthodox like St. Francis of Assisi, have led the Church to the
realization that its human component cannot fully assimilate
their notions of perfection. Because the Church is human it is
perforce weak and sinful. A perfect Church in the present
dispensation could not exist because it would *ipso facto* become an idol; it would itself become a matter of ultimate concern. Some of the Fathers of the Church dwell on St. Paul's
description of how God chose to deal with men. He selected
the weak and poor things of this world, the seemingly inept
persons and means for his work: not Marcus Aurelius the

philosopher-emperor, but the poor carpenter's son; not Seneca, but the fisherman Peter. To point up this idea some maintained that Christ must have been a very ugly, repulsive person as far as his physical appearance is concerned. It really is not fair to question just the Church of our own times about its failings. If we assume a highly critical attitude, we must question Christ himself. Was not Judas' question about the poor a valid one? What did Christ do or say about one of the greatest social abuses of his time, slavery? We must question the apostles. Did not St. John author a Gospel that for centuries was used to justify a cruel, blind and relentless anti-Semitism in the Church? Did not Paul's Pharisaical zeal lay upon the backs of the Gentiles burdens commensurate with those he lifted from the shoulders of Jews?

Those who cannot abide a difference between doctrine and practice in the Church and are tempted to leave it might well ponder the words of a modern evangelist: "If you find a perfect Church, then by all means join it! But mark you well: from that time on it will no longer be perfect!"

To those priests who can really appreciate what the incarnation and all that it implies signify in their lives the humanity of the Church will not be seen so much as an obstacle to faith as a demand for love. Precisely because it is so human, the Church has need for the concern, the efforts at understanding and the basic trust of its membership, particularly of its priests. Precisely because it is so human is the Church so lovable. If some priests today find the Church best described in the words of Savonarola as a harlot, then maybe their mission is the same as that of Osee the prophet.

As Christ predicted, scandals there are in the Church, and scandals there will always be. But through the power of the Spirit, the Church of our time seems to be changing for the better. And change presents a challenge, a challenge which can make being a priest today an exciting and thrilling thing. The reform that the Church is experiencing is ensuring in it a better realization of Gospel values. The Church is taking the first steps toward the realization in itself of that image projected by Vatican II. It is emphasizing more and more its role of service to mankind. It is starting to reorganize some of its structures in the light of that objective. The image of Christ washing the feet of his disciples is becoming ever more discernible in it. But never more than at that moment when it begins more clearly to apprehend itself as identified with Christ, with his job to do in the world, is its faith put to the test.

CHAPTER V
The Professional Knowledge of the Priest

Today great stress is laid, especially in seminaries, on the professionalism of the priest. His service role to mankind is emphasized. Pastoral programs are proliferated, clinical contacts established, and internship courses set up. Yet all the skills inculcated in these programs, if they are truly professional ones, must be grounded in an integrated body of knowledge. For the professional in the traditional sense is one who serves others with his special knowledge, knowledge which is extensive and yet synthesized, knowledge which can promote the physical, mental and spiritual well-being of fellow humans. In history the classical professions were those of the physician, the lawyer and the minister. These men dedicated and devoted themselves to the cultivation of that field of knowledge which would help them serve others: medicine, law and theology. That is why they were called professionals. If today's priest is regarded as a professional, it will not be merely because of the clinical programs he has participated in; it will be because of his knowledge and use of theology.

It is well known that doctors receive about twelve years of medical education and training. But because science is forever uncovering new data and new techniques are often proving successful, a doctor's education is never complete. He must continue to apply himself to his schooling by reading professional literature, attending conventions and involving himself in hospital staff meetings. Lawyers too must keep abreast of the continually changing legal scene. Every day brings them new juridical decisions and new interpretations of the law. It is quite obvious that the lawyer cannot succeed in his profession unless he keeps in contact with the sources which supply needed information. But recent surveys would tend to indicate that priests in general do not keep in contact with the media of theological education. Many dioceses sponsor continuing education programs, and some require all their priests to attend. But these programs rarely run for more than three or four days a year, and, at that, attempt to cover all areas of theological development. Considering the fact that the serious professional theological journals can account for a number of subscribers representing much less than 10 per cent of all the priests in the country, one would conclude that necessary theological updating does not take place through reading either. Undoubtedly there are many reasons for this extraordinary phenomenon in a group of highly trained persons who consider themselves to be professionals. But the two most commonly alleged are that there can really be no substantially new development in orthodox theology since it is an expression of faith and the truths of faith can never change; and, secondly, that the people to whom the priest must minister are comfortable with traditional views, and any attempt to modify them would only result in confusion, divisions and dissension in the parishes.

As it has been taught in the past, theology, or at least systematic theology, has been reduced to a series of theses or propositions upon which judgment is to be passed. Take, for instance, the following five propositions; in the light of your theological training make a judgment as to whether they are true or false with respect to Catholic teaching:

1. Everyone should be free to accept and profess that faith which his own conscience demands.
2. Men can save their souls in any religious group or ecclesial community.
3. It would not be good today to have Catholicism as a state religion.
4. Taking away political power from the Church would greatly facilitate its freedom to pursue its real mission.
5. The Roman pontiff ought to reconcile himself with the progress, liberalism and secularity of the modern world.

If you considered every one of these propositions to be false your theological status would have been excellent one hundred years ago, for every one of the propositions was condemned by the famous syllabus of errors published with the Bull *Quanta cura* by Pope Pius IX in 1864. But obviously not all of the propositions can be considered false today. Vatican II and papal documents of our own time clearly espouse some of these ideas, as for instance, the freedom of the individual to follow his own conscience in matters of faith.

Again ponder some of these theological positions championed in the past by the highest authority in the Church and see if they are tenable today:

The Blood of Jesus Christ cries out against Jews! Christians may not kill them because the divine law forbids murder. But they should be made to wander homeless on the face of the earth until they are filled with shame, and brought to confess the name of Jesus Christ, the Lord. How can Christian leaders aid or assist blasphemers of the name of Christ in oppressing the servants of the Lord? Should they not instead force them into servitude, into that slavery of which they made themselves deserving when they raised sacrilegious hands against Him who had come to confer true liberty upon them, and called down his blood upon themselves and their children.
Innocent III, thirteenth century: Bull *Ut esset Cain*.

The mayor or city council is hereby ordered to force all captured heretics to confess their crime and accuse all their accomplices. He shall do this by the application of such torture as will not imperil life or do permanent damage to limb.

> Innocent IV, thirteenth century: Bull *Ad extirpanda*.

Anyone pertinaciously presuming to defend the error that it is not sinful to take money for the loan of money is, we hereby decree, to be punished as a heretic would be punished.

> Clement V, fourteenth century: Constitution *Ex gravi ad nos*.

The sun is the center about which the world revolves. —This is a proposition foolish and absurd in philosophy and formally heretical, inasmuch as it expressly contradicts expressions found in Holy Scripture in many places according to the proper sense of the words and the common explanation and interpretation of the Holy Fathers and learned theologians.

> Holy Office of the Inquisition, seventeenth century: Condemnation of Galileo.

In the lands conquered by Alphonse, the King of Portugal, and the Enfante Henry, many people from Guinea as well as other Negroes are being held in captivity. Other Negroes too are being taken to these lands because they have been purchased as slaves either by legitimate contract or by an exchange of articles not considered contraband. A goodly number of these slaves have already been converted to the Catholic faith. So we hope that the divine clemency will prosper the continuation of this project until either the whole people is converted or at least many more souls are won for Christ. . . . But we have heard that some Christians are thwarting the efforts of said King and his Enfante . . . by supplying contraband materials through which these enslaved peoples are able to become stronger and resist more fiercely. This, we declare, cannot be done without serious offense to God and grave insult to the whole of the Christian world. . . . Since we have granted with our apostolic authority to Alphonse and his successors the right to invade, conquer, destroy, make war against and subjugate these lands and reduce

> their peoples to perpetual slavery . . . we want it known that no other Christian has any right whatsoever without the permission of the said King to interfere in this project. . . . Should anyone do so, besides the penalties he might incur for giving arms to Mohammedans, he would fall automatically under the sentence of excommunication.
>
> Nicholas V, fifteenth century: Bull *Romanus Pontifex*

These statements make it all too clear that the Church and its theology cannot be regarded as a little parcel of heaven fallen down upon the earth. Like the human beings who make it up, the Church and the doctrine it inculcates are subject to the laws of historical development, and are at one and the same time both conditioned by the consciousness and understandings of the era and wide open to continual possibilities of transcendence. The Church has always been regarded as a living organism, dependent upon its environment, yet capable of adaptation and evolution. Without an appreciation of the historicity of the consciousness of the Church, we would tend to be harsh on popes like Innocent III, Innocent IV and Nicholas V. Judging them by what we know today about the true meaning of the Gospel, we would instantly repudiate what they taught in the documents quoted above. But with an appreciation of the possibility of theological development, we would see how unjust such a judgment would be. For as historical beings, they like us, could only function in accordance with the knowledge, understanding, appreciation, value systems and feelings of their own time.

To be sure, Vatican I taught: "If anyone should say that it might happen that as science progresses, another sense might be attributed to dogma than that which the Church has meant and means, let him be anathema." If dogma is apprehended to mean the primary concretization of faith in fundamental propositions, one might be tempted to interpret the Council to mean that at least these primary principles cannot change, that at least such fundamental formulations of the faith cannot be subject to the vagaries of historical development. One might dare to say that there can be no such thing as evolution of dogma. But, of course, the Council could not mean that. What is meant, as the traditional theology has always proposed, is that only those understandings of dogma that have been received in the Church and are being received by the magisterium of the Church are to be regarded as authentic. What is stated is not that there can be no development of doctrine, but that there can be no development of dogma apart from development in the Church. The very fact that not only the past tense of the verb (has meant) but also the present (means) is used marks an acknowledgment of the historicity of the Church, and does not necessarily imply that present meanings are exactly the same as past ones. All that is taught is that in whatever era dogmatic development occurs, it is to be regarded as authentic only if it takes place under the guidance of magisterial authority.

The possibility of doctrinal development has been acknowledged often in pronouncements of the magisterium. Pius XII, for instance, in a talk given to Roman theological students in 1939, stated: "We thoroughly approve and recommend that the ancient wisdom be brought into accord, if need be, with the new discoveries of scholarship." Again in his encyclical *Humani generis* he indicates another source of development: "Each font of divinely revealed doctrine contains so many rich treasures of truth that they can never be exhausted." So also Pope Paul VI in his profession of faith noted: "The Church, most assuredly, has always the duty to carry on the effort to study more deeply and to present in a manner even better adapted to successive generations the unfathomable mysteries of God, rich for all in the fruits of salvation. But at the same time the greatest care must be taken, while fulfilling the indispensable duty of research, to do no injury to the teachings of Christian doctrine." The bishops of the provinces of Baltimore and Washington in a letter to their priests remarked: "Theology apparently is embarking upon a period of renewal which may prove as promising and exciting as that of the sacred liturgy. Instead of merely repeating what others have said in the past, today's theologians are grappling with new problems, asking new questions, and using new techniques to discover answers. They have at their disposal resources which were not available to their predecessors. There is nothing wrong or even unusual about this—they are simply doing for our day what the Fathers and Scholastics did for theirs."

It is certainly possible to make some distinction between faith and dogma. Dogma can be conceived of as a basic propositional articulation of the truths of faith. Theology can be viewed as a further development of and reflection upon dogma and an adaptation of it to the understanding and needs of a particular era. Theology, formally considered, is a purely human science. As such it certainly is capable of modification and evolution, and indeed it must be changed if its original content is to be preserved in the context of evolving consciousness, meaning and language.

This is clear when it is kept on a level of theory and abstraction. But the extremely close relationship that exists between theology and the object it studies, dogma and the data of revelation, often makes this distinction difficult of application in the concrete. Never have the truths of faith existed in some absolute and pure form, distinct and apart from the modalities of human thought and expression. Faith exists concretely in propositions. No religious truth is completely free from the trammels of some kind of theology, howsoever simple and rudimentary that might be, for to exist truth must be understood. It has to be given an interpretation in the light of the consciousness of the time in which it is formulated. Only by giving it some kind of interpretation can man take possession of the truth, and in turn be possessed by it. Without some previous understanding it is not possible to understand. This is a simple and yet paramount finding of modern psychology. One cannot understand music unless one is to a certain extent already musical. One cannot make sense out of a book of pure mathematics unless one has already learned in some crude way at least to think mathematically. So one cannot really possess a truth of faith unless one has learned at least in some rudimentary fashion to think theologically. So faith has to be in some way dependent upon theology. And indeed faith can vary as theologies vary. Wherever there is need for interpretation, myriad meanings and reflections are possible to men of different upbringing and background, in varying cultural and educational milieux.

So it is that not even the revelation that we have in the Bible exists in some kind of pure and absolute form. No thinking man has ever viewed the Bible as a kind of letter fallen down from heaven or dictated by God to his agents on earth. Every word in the Bible reflects the philosophy, thought and value system of a particular people at a definite time of their cultural evolution. Every thought is couched in the modalities of interpretation and understanding indigenous to a definite concrete situation. The so-called *Sitz im Leben* has become for the modern Scripture scholar the key to arriving at the essential message given by God to men in his dealings with them. It is only through the word of man that one can arrive at the word of God. This, admittedly, is a tenuous and risky way of proceeding. But the fact is that God has chosen to deal with man in this way. And faith was never meant to be easy. It demands much more of a sacrifice than, perhaps, is commonly understood, for it requires not merely an acceptance of what God has revealed, but to a certain extent, an acceptance also of the vehicle of that revelation. Faith in the final analysis really presupposes the abandonment of all human security in knowing. A security-blanket type of theology would not actually be working in the service of faith, but at cross-purposes with it.

So through the course of history this initial theology, this biblical theology which is our closest point of contact with the divine and which is leagued most intimately with the ultimate source of our faith, was adapted and developed, tooled and honed to the understanding of successive generations of Christians. It was fitted upon a series of latticeworks to be more easily grasped and contemplated by peoples of different eras and cultural backgrounds. It was given a *Gestalt*, a structure, a philosophical setting which rendered it more accessible to various peoples and thus more capable of memorialization. The better the process of acculturation worked among a particular people, under the guidance of the Spirit, to be sure, the more Christian they became.

After New Testament times the data of revelation passed through Gnostic hands to the Platonists, for whom, contrary to our views, the material world was not the real one at all, but only a shadow, a reflection, a symbol of it. For the Platonist Fathers the only reality was and had to be spiritual. Their doctrine, for instance, on the Eucharist, epitomized so well by Ratram of Corbie, might well be considered heretical if judged by modern standards. For they could not hold an identity between the Eucharistic body of Christ and his historical one. Christ's presence in the Eucharist was real because it was a spiritual presence. The historical, material body of Christ, on the other hand, was merely a symbol of who and what he was. The only relationship that could exist between the Eucharistic and historical body was the one that exists between a reality that is symbolized and the symbol representing it. Eventually this view changed; it had to change because evolution is part and parcel of human existence. In some quarters that evolution went too far. The Platonistic view was completely reversed: the Eucharistic body became merely a symbol of the real, historical body. But heresy can

emanate from refusal to change as easily as from exaggerated
change. In history many became heretics precisely because of
their devotion to traditional formulas. They were unable to
grasp the fact that old formulations, sufficient for one generation, could become quite inadequate for another. This might
have occurred even in Testamental times, for it seems that
the Gospel of St. John was written to offset the teaching of
heretics who resented the promulgation of the message of
Christ in Greek thought forms rather than Hebrew ones at a
time when, as a matter of fact, more pagans were apparently
being converted than Jews. The sacrosanct and tradition formula of St. Cyril of Alexandria relative to the question of
Monophysitism: "The one nature of the incarnate God," became heretical when conservative elements in the Church refused to change their understanding of it after the Council of
Chalcedon. Jansenists abhorred the minimalist position on
charity, still advocating the need of perfect contrition for the
forgiveness of sin after the definition of the Council of Trent.
And so they became heretics.

In the thirteenth century Aristotelianism began to replace
Platonism. And it has dominated Catholic theology up until
very recently. Its bent was to objectify. Its aim was to be
scientific. Emphasis shifted from subject to object, from a
spiritual archetype to a material one, from persons to things,
from the inner to the outer. Ultimately it culminated in the
highly defined Cartesian distinction between the subjective
and objective. In the Aristotelian system metaphysics was
simply physics purified by further abstraction. For the Stagi-
rite such a reality as personality was not fully comprehensible,
and consequently of no great philosophical importance. It
could be understood only as an adjunct of nature or essence
rendering it concrete in the individual. The one could be
fully apprehended only in terms of the many, the concrete in
terms of the abstract, reality in terms of essence. A being in
flux as such would be totally unknowable. The points of de-

parture and arrival in change could alone provide polarities upon which the mind could be fixed. To be being had really to be static. The less a being was subject to change the more perfect it was considered in the order of being. Aristotle's accent was on mechanics and justice in the world of change. Each individual was viewed as a self-contained mechanism essentially able to achieve its purpose; conscious beings might not have at their immediate disposal all that they could project as necessary for their well-being, or attainment of their goal; they then would acquire the right to obtain the means from others. Since nature was considered an absolute and being static, so truth had to be irrelative and permanent, for truth could be nothing more than the conformity of mind to the reality of nature and being. Truth could be attained most perfectly when the mind attends to unchanging essences or natures. The semantics of the system allowed only for a literal or metaphorical understanding of words in relation to thoughts and corresponding essences.

Aristotelianism was laid to rest by Kantianism, by subjectivism and the modern philosophies which emanated from it, philosophies in better accord with the empirical findings of current psychology. With the demise of Aristotelianism the pendulum swung back again toward the spiritual, the subjective, the personal. To be sure, this new movement did not represent a recrudescence of Platonism. The pattern that emerged is more like a fulfillment of the Hegelian dialectic. Newer philosophies reflected a synthesis which tended to break down the absolute dichotomy that had been postulated between the subjective and the objective. Reality can be grasped by man only in terms of the meaning he attaches to it. What as a matter of fact is must be significant to someone in order to exist as far as he is concerned. An object represented in one's mind inasmuch as it is represented belongs to the sphere of the subjective. To represent the mind does not, as Aristotle contended, become all things; it must forever remain mind.

The philosophical pluralism of our era makes for confusion. The newer systems agree only in their rejection of the old. They are united only in challenging the validity of the assumption upon which Aristotelianism and Scholasticism are based—the objectivity of metaphysical being, i.e., a being which lies beyond the phenomenological universe and the sciences which attempt to categorize and explain it, a being therefore that lies beyond the physical, and yet is not purely intentional, a creation of the mind; metaphysical being is conceived of as one possessing properties belonging to both the physical and intentional orders, a being whose essence can be comprehended, but whose existence has to be demonstrated. These new philosophies reject the analogy of being, the concept which lies at the core of Scholasticism. What are these philosophies? There is personalism, which considers man in his subjectivity as the hub around which all philosophy must revolve. Historicism views the cultural development of humanity as the key to the understanding of all reality. Existentialism invites man to employ his freedom to make himself exist, rather than just to remain content with being. Process philosophy contemplates change and evolution as the very substance of the universe. Linguistic analysis considers language to be the basic form of human life, words as being prior to thought, and the study of the use of speech as the key to all understanding.

Each succeeding philosophical system implies a shift of emphasis from the polarity stressed in the previous system, or the system against which it specifically reacts, to its counterpart: from object to subject, or from subject-object dichotomy to subject-object identity, from thing to person, from rigidity to flux, from thought to word.

Apart from the gnosiological and noetic implications of these new philosophies for the development of theology as a science, there have been more practical consequences also. Any idea is truly viable only if it influences life. When people lived in the grasp of philosophical orientations whose emphases were upon the many, upon essence and nature, upon mechanics and justice, the individual person was submerged. He experienced his worth as but little more than nothing. He was only a cog in a gigantic juggernaut. He felt threatened and insecure unless he fit himself into the machine. His transcendence of self was seen only in terms of what was bigger than himself. His responsibilities were kept at a minimum by authorities to reduce threat. The leader assumed responsibility. This was the burden of his office. He had to take the weight of decision-making from the shoulders of his subjects. Dostoyevsky at a time when democracy was beginning to influence the world reflected this attitude so well in the scene with the Grand Inquisitor in the *Brothers Karamazov*. Scripture has captured it so poignantly in 2 Kings 13:28ff. when Absalom reassures his henchmen: "Wait till Amnon is bemused with wine. Then when I say: 'Strike!' slay him. Have no fear. You do but execute my orders. Take heart and show yourselves to be men of mettle!" But today's world is too much filled with memories of Dachau and Buchenwald and the Nuremberg trials to accept such a doctrine. Today's world is too much influenced by existentialism, personalism and democratic idealism to believe that an individual's personal responsibility can be so easily alienated. Democracy is too much a goal of today's society to permit belief in the divine right of kings. So today's ethical theology stresses the responsibility of each individual in a decision-making situation and his inalienable right as a Christian, as one freed by Christ from servitude to law, to chart his own course in accordance with his conscience, rightly guided, of course, by the Church's teaching.

Current philosophies, then, suggest that, difficult though it might be in the concrete, it is necessary to distinguish in every articulation of a truth the reality or content of the statement, and its formulation or expressional modality. While the reality or content remains the same, the formulation of the truth about it must forever remain conditioned and only partial. The formulation will be conditioned because it will respond to questions asked, questions arising from particular subjective concerns of people of a particular era, certain geographical location or definite mind-set and culture. And the answers given to the initial questions will in turn raise new questions in the same vein and so on. Thus a definite determinism arising from the pattern of questioning will eventually appear in the systematic treatment of the original reality under discussion. All one has to do is to turn to almost any topic in an encyclopedia to turn up the questions that have in the course of years, as long as the subject has been within the ken of man, appeared as the significant ones. If the question you want answered is totally new, fully different from the ones considered significant in the past, you will not find an answer.

The conditioned formulas of response, however, can both truly represent the reality under discussion, leaving it intact in its unchanging actuality, and though they touch upon the same aspect of that reality, differ widely among themselves because of their accommodation to the understanding, appreciation and value systems of the people for whom they are intended. Take, for example, the value of the American dollar on June 17, 1972. It is a reality, a content, that as far as that date is concerned cannot and does not change. But that value becomes a concrete, perceptible, significant factor to people in other lands only when a formula is offered in response to the question: "What is it worth in our money?" Formulations will have to differ precisely to maintain an identical content, but formulation there will have to be, if any true understanding is to be had. So the dollar, remaining exactly what it is, is .38 pound to the British; 22.96 hellers to the Austrians; 44.03 francs to the Belgians; 5.02 francs to the French; 3.84 francs to the Swiss; 3.17 marks to the West Germans; 7.24 rupees to the Indians; 580.88 lire to the Italians; 303.49 yen to the Japanese; 64.52 pesos to the Spanish. The conditional status of formulation applies to other characteristics than quantity. Suppose a person draws three stick men on a blackboard. With the chalk he colors in the face of one. Then he asks the question: "How many black men are there on the board?" Of course his question cannot be answered without a previous inquiry. The formulation to be made in answer to the initial question will be conditioned upon the answer given to the second question. While the content remains exactly the same, an entirely different answer can be elicited for the first question by giving a different interpretation to the second one.

Any formulation about reality has perforce to be partial. Limitless questions can be asked about the smallest, most commonplace item. Human knowledge can address itself to being only in a piecemeal fashion by prescinding and abstracting. But reality can never be exhausted; the conceptual or notional potential of it will always remain umplumbed simply because new discoveries in other areas will bring new questions to be asked. While the reality remains the same, the formulations about it can increase indefinitely. Take, for instance, the theological issue of heaven. The ancient world was largely concerned with its location. The early Christians placed it in the sky. So they speak of Christ's "ascension" into heaven; of his body rising from earth and disappearing in a cloud, etc. Medieval theology was more interested in its essence. Taken for granted that it was the source of maximum human pleasure and fulfillment, was it fundamentally a total activation of intellect or will? Does it consist essentially in knowledge or love? The theological formulation of the doctrine of the beatific vision supplied the answer to these questions. Today perhaps the most important question that peo-

ple ask about heaven is if it is necessary. Can one get along
without it? Does one have to have a reward to be a good
Christian? Is goodness its own reward? Can I be sufficiently
happy and fulfilled in this life? Theology has only begun to
address itself to these questions. What questions the future
will bring relative to this doctrine will depend not only upon
the answer the present era will give, but also upon the psychological mood, the mind-set and consciousness of the future.

The fact that it is possible to have only a partial formulation of what is contained in the truths of faith as well as the
fact that the formulations that have been made have responded to the mentality and mood of a particular era have
led theologians today to introduce the principle of doctrinal
ecdysis. Certain insects, crustaceans, snakes and other an-
imals periodically shed their outer layer of skin in rather
spectacular fashion. Birds molt. So theology has to shuck off
older formulations which are no longer significant or consonant with the mentality of the age because they responded to the questions of an earlier period, not to current
ones. Of course, this does not mean that these formulations
are no longer true. They most certainly are in the context in
which they evolved. But they no longer exert an influence on
men's lives; they do not supply an answer for the questions
that men now are asking. So they are to be laid to rest in
mothballs. Such a formulation might, of course, revive again
at some future age, when, perhaps, the question which
sparked it initially into existence will be asked again. As
regards this issue, very often liturgical practice will herald
doctrinal ecdysis. Take, for instance, the doctrine of Mary's
immaculate heart. It is a theological formulation that remains
as true today as it was in the past. But it has fallen into
theological desuetude. The feast has been removed from the
calendar. But perhaps some authority or saint in the future

will show its relevance to life as it then will be led. So it will be revived.

There are perhaps more dead theological formulations today than scholars are willing to admit. There are many new questions which research has not as yet been able to answer. But the work of pruning and reformulating can go on only if there is close co-operation between priests involved with people in the parishes and theologians skilled enough to know what can be done without damaging faith and courageous enough to lay aside what has to be shelved. The pastor must supply the new questions his people are asking; the theologian must work out the new formulation of doctrine to respond to them. But such co-operation can be forthcoming only if parish priests become more deeply concerned about their professional knowledge.

The fact is that many Catholics still live by and interpret their faith through formulations that resulted from questions asked in eras whose concerns were quite different from today's. Many of the formulations still in vogue in certain quarters of the Church today originated in the matrix of a medieval mentality that is quite foreign to the prevailing spirit in educated circles today. Young people in particular find it difficult to reconcile this theology, which, perhaps, their parents still profess, with what they learn in the philosophy, history and science courses they take at a university. These young people are the future of the Church. The American Church in particular has always been concerned about their education, and has in the past provided a Catholic educational system ranging from pre-school programs to the university to help them reconcile their theology with other fields. But the system is no longer being sustained in many places, and where it is, the education it offers does not differ substantially from that available in the secular schools.

The irreconcilability of the old and new theological positions has produced an identity crisis, the like of which the

Church has not experienced for many centuries. But one thing is certain. It is the young people who are experiencing its pangs the most. And though many of them are thirsting after authentic religious outlets, they are drifting away from the Church, in which they find relatively few priests who can really appreciate their problems and who are equipped with a relevant, updated professional knowledge such as can be of help to them in answering the questions that arise in their minds. They feel that they can be comfortable only with a Catholic identity that responds to the modern spirit. They can appreciate as helpful in their own lives only that theology which addresses itself to the questions that are significant today and that proceed from bases quite different from those whence the classical theology sprang.

What are the characteristics of this modern spirit? What mentality prevails today in institutions of higher learning? What are the significant moods of youth in our day? What are the signs of the times that current theology has to reckon with if it is still to be considered the professional knowledge of the priest?

The modern spirit is radically secular or this-worldly. It is highly focused upon the present. What is real is what I experience here and now. The past is gone; the future is at best uncertain. The cult of the now is crystallized in both sentience and action. My awareness of the now is heightened by the creation of a constant stream of varying and exciting sensations. Concentration on my sensation helps me forget who I am. Hyperactivity also helps to highlight my awareness of the now. Very often the psyche is poised between the two polarities of hyperactivity on the one hand and passive states of heightened perception induced by drugs or transcendental meditation on the other. A continuing series of psychic ups and downs can also serve to accentuate the present, fleeting moment. But lurking somewhere in the shadows behind this façade is the desire for some kind of future breakthrough. In all of the concentration on the present, one perceives an oblique awareness of both the future and the past. The one who wholeheartedly cultivates the present certainly will not accept responsibility for the future; perhaps it is this thought of responsibility that forces attention to be turned to only the present. But he does harbor the hope that somehow, despite his own insouciance about it, or even perhaps precisely because of his own insouciance about it, a better state of affairs will emerge in the future. Though on the surface there seems to be little overt interest in history on the part of young people today, there are evidences of a covert idealization of it. Many psychologists consider personal styles of dress and grooming among the young to be an indication of a desire to return to the values and consciousness of the past. Beards, levis, simple long dresses and hair styles are all reminiscent of pioneer days. But the cult of the present that masks this idealization of the past betrays a fear of debunking, of the disclosure that the past really was not what it was cracked up to be. The demythologizing tendencies of current scientific history have turned young people off. A suspicion is entertained that what they secretly admire, the heroes and heroines of the past with their personal strength, highly defined self-awareness, purposefulness and moral rectitude, will be destroyed by the penetrating gaze of scientific historical research. So a double message is given. On the level of secondary consciousness the desire to keep the past as it was and to try to keep it alive as it was even in the present is manifested in dress and life-style. On the level of primary consciousness there is a denial of the importance of the past, and a protestation of the fact that only the present really matters.

A second characteristic of the modern spirit as found in young people today is that it is highly egocentric and introverted. The issue of personal identity is paramount. Who am I? Why am I I and not someone else? How is my personality tied in with my consciousness? What are my responsibilities

to myself, to my fellow men, to future men, to my environment, to God, if he exists? Am I really accountable for my
actions? Psychologists report that there is among young people an increasingly characteristic negative self-definition. People tend to identify themselves in terms of what they do not
have. They express themselves through estrangement, rejection, protest, anger. They tend generally to accentuate the
negative in all aspects of their lives. They do not feel able to
commit themselves to anything; they see commitment as loss
of integrity and freedom. Yet, contrariwise, they view freedom
as a terrible burden: to be free is to be accountable. Many
refuse both to accept the adult burden of freedom on the one
hand and to submit to authority on the other. They prefer
just to hang loose and wait for something to happen. Some
rebel against the establishment, yet have no desire to commit
themselves to any revolutionary cause. Dedication of oneself
to the established way of life is often interpreted as a cop-out.
There is manifested a great deal of fear and suspicion of acculturation. In the ultimate analysis what is most desired, a
strong, highly integrated, identifiable personality, is precisely
what is lost by diffusion and lack of ability to accept or im-
pose any type of organizational factor. Perhaps it is a basic
inability to identify the self that gives rise to an almost in-
satiable thrust toward self-expression. The desire to be oneself and to be able to identify that self gives rise to the need
to wear many masks in public, to be seen in them, to observe
through the reaction of others which one would feel most
comfortable.

Undoubtedly it is the confusion about self that gives rise
to a third characteristic of the modern spirit, its emphasis
upon interpersonal relationships. Being with others as much
as possible is almost a *sine qua non* of modern existence.
Doing things together is the only way. Solitude, loneliness,
aloofness are the only great evils that the modern youth culture abhors. Yet here too a certain ambivalence crops out.

There is a great need for others both to help in the process of self-definition and identification and to supply what is lacking to the self, to complete and bring to maturity the potentials for development and expression that each individual possesses. But on the other hand there are indications of an uneasiness, of an untoward anxiety about the self being lost, being submerged in a welter of interpersonal activity or in too great a concentration of efforts on pleasing and helping others. Uncertainty is manifested about the possibility of striking a balance between fulfillment of the urge for self-development and the drive toward altruism and the cultivation of highly meaningful and rewarding personal relationships with others. Love of self and love of others become confused and create personal problems that cannot be resolved in the case of those who manifest antipathy toward organization and structure of any kind.

The modern spirit betrays a mistrust of system, yet it is yearning for the positive values and goals that systems can provide. The highly functional and pragmatic systems of the business world are not rejected, certainly, by those who devote themselves to such pursuits. But a distinction is often made between livelihood and living. While by dint of circumstances one might be forced into a system to survive, no analogy can be drawn from this practical exigency for a more realistic view of life itself. One phase of existence need not influence others. While one can be highly structured in his business operations, the rest of his life might be, of set purpose, in total disarray. Of equal pragmatic value with a means of livelihood is education. Here again a system, a structure, is cultivated for its own sake, for the advantage it can offer to the individual and society. The modern spirit strives above all to be realistic. And so as it must acknowledge a need for organization in business, it must also credit educational systems with some value. Though it cultivates no integrated philosophy, no particular *Weltanschauung* itself, the modern spirit really owes much to today's scientific and philosophical attitudes. For it arises from the principles cultivated by science and philosophy today, principles that are diametrically opposed to values inculcated in past systems.

What are some of these principles? What is the attitude of science and philosophy today? What values are considered as paramount today in higher educational circles? How do these differ from those entertained in the past?

The first principle is that people today, in every aspect of their existence, will have to learn to live with and be satisfied with the tentative. Our knowledge today cannot be comfortably certain. The ancient world valued what the Greek philosophers called *epistēmē*, certain and true knowledge. The modern world can lay claim only to *doxa*, a high degree of probability. Today's science knows very well that it is not possible to verify all the interrelated aspects of reality empirically at one and the same time. We do not have measuring instruments adequate to the task. Even if logical argument proceeds by way of necessity and consequently could result in absolutely true and certain conclusions, the premises it would have to use would be based upon empirical data. Given only a high degree of probability in the data in the premises one could not expect any kind of certainty in the conclusion. Then too, while modern science may still speak of cause and effect, it certainly does not acknowledge a principle of causality understood in the medieval sense. It is much more comfortable with speaking of statistical concomitance than with an inner relationship of necessity. It will always acknowledge the fact that, given a sufficient number of attempts, unexpected results may be obtained from well-known causes. This principle founds the evolutionary hypothesis upon which all science today relies. And it makes all scientific knowledge, though practically reliable and workable in billions and billions of applications, only tentative in the final analysis.

Secondly, finality was very much a principle of life in the ancient and medieval world. While it still is cultivated in certain pragmatic situations, as, for instance, in business, in today's world it has ceased to be for many an important principle of life. Today's spirit is basically ateleological. It prepares people to accept the idea that life is not and need not be necessarily fully meaningful. It highlights the significance of mystery and paradox. It points up the meaningfulness of meaninglessness. It humbles man. Despite all his scientific and technological progress he has not been able to assign a significant purpose to life itself. In fact, science very often stresses the prodigious waste of life and life potential that abounds everywhere on earth. Life does not have to have a goal. Everything does not have to have an explanation. Man must curb the penchant he feels to create meaning. If he is to make real progress, his mind must cease to project its own need for organization and order and purposefulness upon the universe. Man will be better off psychologically and intellectually if he learns how to live without meaning.

A third principle for the understanding of the modern world is that of relativity. Nothing is to be considered absolute. Reality, at least as it is apprehended by the human mind, does not exist in and by itself in total independence from other reality. All being is dependent and conditioned. All being is interconnected. The mind apprehends things the way it does because sense percepts report reality as interrelated. And in the mind itself interpretation has to be involved with interpretation, truth with truth, judgment with judgment, idea with idea so that an intricate concatenation of mental images results in which each component can stand by itself only because it is supported by its nearest fellows in the complex structure. The general and special theories of relativity, introduced into physics by Albert Einstein decades ago, have had their effect upon philosophy, psychology and noetics.

The fourth principle is that of personalism. Whereas past perspectives have limelighted societies, institutions and organizations, today's attention is riveted on the individual. The human person is the zenith of the evolutionary process that is in evidence in the world. All reality must be interpreted, evaluated and ranked in relation to its usefulness to the human person. The individual human being is the center and hub of all reality. The new consciousness is very much aware of that fact. Each individual is unique; each is free; each must be allowed to do his thing unhampered by the unnecessary strictures imposed by society. The new consciousness protests against organizations which have subverted, distorted and caricaturized the spirit of *Gemeinschaft* that once prevailed in human society and converted it into a *Gesellschaft* in which the individual is submerged and smothered in a host of rules and regulations issued "for the common good" (*ad bonum commune*). Freedom is primarily the property of the individual; only if its individual members are free can a society be free. Organizations tend to stifle freedom; they must immolate the individual to attain their goals. The human person is crushed in the juggernaut of the military-industrial complex, of numberless businesses that supply him with the necessities of life at a price that he can hardly pay, of government itself which under the pretext of affording him security, protection and assistance often takes in taxes of one kind or another the lion's share of his earnings. The new consciousness is disturbed at all of this. It is aware of the dictum of John Stuart Mill that whatever crushes individuality is despotism, by whatever name it may be called. When the Church casts itself in the image of an organization modeled after the state, when moreover it arrogates to itself powers even greater than those of any state, when it appears as transhistorical, immutable, omniscient, impeccable, invested with absolute and supreme divine authority, when it becomes a surrogate for God, an idol, and when its chief defensive mechanism is perceived to be secrecy, it becomes a prime target for the new consciousness. The mind of youth cannot see how such a juggernaut could be the creation of the Christ, the "little flock" of the humble, open, honest, authentic, loving guru of Nazareth. The credibility gap is too great.

Fifthly, the modern spirit recognizes the world as processive. The final state has not yet arrived. Reality is not finished, but to be completed. Everything, some things obviously more than others, is in motion; everything is being modified; everything is being changed. It is the human task to interpret and give meaning to process: to judge whether change be beneficial or deleterious; it is man's job to aid and abet those processes that are beneficial, as well as to alter or divert those that are harmful. Man, realizing his place in the process of nature, will not pollute his environment, but will promote natural development as he sees that it is beneficial for life as he knows it. An awareness of process prevents man from interpreting the condition of the world as it is now as the permanent, final one. Consequently it makes him more aware of his responsibilities for the future. The phase of the process that he is experiencing now will be in large part the determinant of what future generations will have to cope with during their phase of the process. Moreover, earth's processive movement is not cyclic, as perhaps some philosophers of history might intimate. It is ruthlessly rectilinear. What is past will never return; opportunities missed will never present themselves again. Each moment, each now, must be seized and cultivated for the precious link that it is in forging a better and more productive world for the future.

Sixthly, the new consciousness focuses upon autonomy. The most precious endowment of man is his freedom. Older consciousnesses were heteronomous. Perhaps in those times men were like children. They liked to be rid of the burdens that freedom imposes. In return for a reasonably secure and comfortable life they were willing to surrender their freedom to leaders who could make decisions for them and provide for "the common good." Through a formalized regulative system authority could both keep itself informed of the whims and vagaries of its charges, and them apprised of the provisions of law to remedy such contraproductive behavior. The new autonomous individual wants to be treated as a person, not as a cog in a machine. He wants his leader to know him, and in turn wants personally to know the leader. He wants communication to flow in all directions. He wants to have a voice in the decisions taken by the group to which he belongs, and wants all decisions to be group decisions. He wants to feel that he really belongs to the group, that he is accepted by it, that he has a contribution to make to it, that he has a part in directing its future. He wants to see its leader more as a facilitator, as one who has the natural talents to really hear what people are saying, who can help them articulate their feelings, who can perceive common elements in seemingly divergent opinions, synthesize them and win consensus from others in approving of them. In a word, he wants freedom for himself and others, with only such minimal restriction as is necessary for the guarantee of everyone's liberty imposed not from above, but by consensus of the group itself.

The seventh characteristic of the new consciousness is one that seems paradoxical in the light of the foregoing. Though the modern spirit is tentative, ateleological, autonomous, personal, processive and relational, it seems to be engaged in a quest of the absolute and ultimate. Though it pretends to be very realistic, the new consciousness is not above idealism. It seems to be hoping for the impossible. The very things that its core philosophy rejects are those for which it seems to be searching. And the inconsistency which it exhibits is cloaked in a kind of schizoid mental mechanism. A distinction is made between the scientific and the occult. By its own admission science does not claim to know everything. The occult can grope for that which the scientific pronounces as

unlikely (not impossible, to be sure; that would be too apodic-
tic for science). Primitive human cravings for ultimacy and
absoluteness even today betray themselves at times from under the façade of scientific detachment that generally characterizes the spirit of our age.

The modern mentality has been instrumental in whatever
reshaping of the theological enterprise has already been
achieved in our time. The professional knowledge of the
priest is undergoing a retooling to make it a handier, more
serviceable vehicle of information and help. Medieval theology responded to the needs of its own time. Its emphases
were upon philosophy and tradition. Scholasticism emerged
as an excellently integrated rational plan, neatly packaging
both scientific and religious truths. It provided the intellectual
with a means of escape both from law and authority. It
recognized the right of the expert to dissent even from the
most solemn pronouncements of the ecclesial magisterium.
Canon law, on the other hand, as the epitome of tradition,
provided superb guidelines for ordinary priests and people.
It proposed easily understood norms for every action, and
bolstered them with the doctrine that the authority that
stood behind them and sanctioned them was one conceded
to his Church by Jesus himself.

Current theological trends evidence a return to biblical
foundations, emphasis upon the fact of an ongoing revelation through the presence of the Spirit in the Church, and a
general upgrading of the importance of religious feeling in
the Christian community. These trends represent, in part, the
response of theologians to the demands of the new consciousness.

The very factors which seemed to lead medieval theologians
away from too great a reliance on the Bible in their formulations and to fuller dependence upon philosophical arguments
are the ones which are attracting modern scholars aware of
the new consciousness. The Bible is warm, experiential, hu-

man and personal. It is simple and yet so mysterious. It is
tentative and yet contains an aura of the absolute. It proclaims freedom, and links man to God and his fellows with
love. True, it is a record of what happened in the past. But
it is too sacred to be debunked. And it is brought into the
now by the liturgy which dramatizes its texts and captures
its numinosity for all generations.

The idea of God's continuing communication with man
through the Spirit is also one which grabs people today.
Pentecostalism is becoming a subject of interest for theologians. Although pneumatology has certainly been one of the
less developed areas of theology, and there has been very
little consideration of charismatic gifts apart from those enjoyed by the institutional Church, a new biblical and theological personalism is developing. The image of God in every
man, the Christian as another Christ, the task of the believer
in the world today, the right of the layman to express himself—these are all theological notions that suggest that Jesus
and his Spirit are active in all quarters of the Church today;
and these are all notions that are current in theological circles,
and their currency is owing to the fact that they are real issues for the "now" generation in its struggle to know Jesus
and its own relationship to him. The "Jesus movement" and
the "Jesus people" bring relevancy to the old theological issue
of Christ's ongoing revelation of himself in his followers, and
offer a challenge to more traditional, institutionalized Christian groups to explore theologically the charismatic elements
of their religious heritage.

Thirdly, there is a tendency today to bypass the older, rational approach to God and religion, and to rely much more
on both feeling and experience in general. The issue of the
existence of God ceases to be a problem for a person who experiences him. The tendency to highlight feeling and experience blends well with the general trend not only to promote
Christian unity, but also to realize and appreciate better the

fact that all men, Christian and non-Christian alike, hold many values in common. Reason can often provoke disagreement and division. Commonly experienced human sentiment can frequently unite people, or at least create sympathy and empathy. And theology is coming to acknowledge more and more today the fact that the Christian faith is, as a matter of fact, one founded upon religious experience, not upon logic, science or philosophy. It was initially engendered by a theophany we call Jesus. And that theophany sacralized not only all humanity, but the universe itself, and did away with every distinction that pre-Christian man had established between the sacred and the secular. The impulse toward fusion, the desire to be with others, to have all mankind sharing and experiencing that love which lies at the very heart of the message of Jesus at least in some rudimentary way nurtures the very core of the concept of anonymous Christianity which is so important for theology today.

Under the influence of these trends the theology of the past decade can show a number of rather significant accomplishments. First, there has been some successful resolution of the problem of secularization. In its most radical form this movement appeared as Orestean theology. But the news that God is dead no longer stirs people today. They smile and continue on their way to church. Then too, those theologians who were hoping that the Church would dissolve as an organization by being absorbed in the post-Christian era into secular culture have been disappointed. Like God, the Church too still gives evidence of being very much alive, and it continues to do its own thing. But secularization has made some impact upon theology; it has not been completely rejected. The value in it has been preserved in two trends in current theology. Writers today seem comfortable with the idea that theology ought to let the people of God be men and women of their own time; that is, it is not right in the name of religion either to force people to assume a medieval mentality in order to function properly in this area of their lives or else so to separate religious truth and activity from every other human endeavor as to subtly create a new kind of gnosticism. Again, the call of modern theology for the humanizing of ecclesial structures is another of the results of the drift toward the secular. The fact is that due to these trends in theology people are better able to integrate their religion with other facets of their lives today than they ever were in the recent past, and the Church is rejecting the triumphalism of the past and modifying its structures to take into account more the rights and feelings of people.

Secondly, theology is able to show some concrete achievements in the area of ecumenism. Statements of agreement between theologians representing Protestant churches and Catholicism have been issued with reference to Eucharistic doctrine. Other areas of theology are currently being explored. As was stated, some general agreement on the question of Anglican orders has been reached by representative theologians, and their findings have been escalated to the administrative level. A new appreciation of the many points of convergence in Roman Catholic and certain Protestant theological positions has resulted in shared seminary classrooms by the groups involved. Courses relating to biblical science, Church history, pastoral theology and ministerial skills as well as internship programs are commonly offered in an ecumenical setting in the various denominational cluster groups that are fast becoming representative of the theological seminary today.

A third practical consequence of the new theology is the contact it has made with the Marxist left, particularly in France. There is no doubt that this breakthrough has occurred because of the theology of hope developed by the German theologians Moltmann and Pannenberg and adopted by Marxist thinkers like Ernst Bloch. The revolutionary feeds upon the same human sentiments as the Christian. He must have faith in his cause: really believe it into existence. He must be concerned about his comrades; love them, support them, help them, protect them. He must be honest and sincere. He must work for justice. He must sacrifice himself for the good of the party. But above all he must have hope. Without hope of success, without a hope that spurs its protagonists to action, the revolution is doomed. Just as the attention of the revolutionary theorists has been riveted upon the key element of hope, so also has the gaze of the Christian theologian. For both have perceived man's desperate need for hope in an agonizing world situation. The fragmentation of Christian identity that has been considered to have resulted from too great a fixation upon faith in the past has been challenged by the ecumenical movement. Christians may not as yet be able to share a common faith; they have always at least been encouraged by the principles of their own belief to live together in charity. What the theology of our era has discovered is that they are united in hope, not only among themselves, but also with many non-believers.

If the present trends in theology continue, it might be possible to predict what the professional knowledge of the priest of the future will look like. While medieval theology developed largely in the matrix of a single philosophical system, the theology of the immediate future will be wedded to many different philosophical systems. Eventually it will have to seek integration and verification in that one area of the educational enterprise that remains stable, credible, universal and progressive: science. Science will become the matrix of the theology of the future, just as philosophy was the matrix of the theology of the past.

Secondly, the theology of the past tended to be mystadelic; that is, it was geared to provide rational explanations, which, if they did not do away with the mysteries of religion, at least made them more acceptable to the human reason. Thus, for instance, the notion of transubstantiation makes it easier for the Aristotelian mind to accept the mystery of Christ's presence in the Eucharist. On the contrary, the theology of the future, if it is to respond to the needs of young people, will be mystagogic; that is, it will lead men to the mysteries of religion, and encourage them to plunge into the unknown without the solace of rational explanation. So in the future theology will recapture a quality which graced it in many areas during the early development of the Church. It will serve as an introduction to the great mysteries of the Christian life, not as an explanation of them.

Through the efforts of Rudolf Bultmann the present generation of theologians has understood its task as largely one of demythologization. The supposition is that God's revelation to man assumes in great part the form of myth precisely because it inculcates otherworldly realities. For the theologian, of course, myth is not fairy tale. It is not fabricated truth. For Bultmann myth is the only human device that can objectify otherworldly reality in this world. Myth contains the truth of God's world and makes it real insofar as that is possible in this world. The task of theology is to extract from the cultural encrustment of the myth the essence of the truth conveyed by it. But since, as we have said, every formulation of a truth is itself historical and culturally situated, if only by the language that is used to express it, it too stands in need of continuous updating. And since it stands in an abstract and quasi-scientific form, it needs to be concretized in order to be a handy tool for the minister to use with people. In other words, it needs remythologization, in myths more comprehensible to a modern audience. This task of remythologization is, as a matter of fact, often accomplished in the examples and stories used in the sermons and homilies of preachers. But in order to achieve more accurate translation, it may well seem to the theologians of the future to be one of their essential tasks so that the priests whom they serve will have a truly effective professional knowledge with which to minister to people.

Prognosticators of the future of religion are almost unanimous in predicting a greater tendency toward pluralism. They do not see the possibility of any kind of universal world religion emerging even in the somewhat remote future. There seems to be little prospect of the ecumenical movement's attainment of complete unity among Christians in the foreseeable future; at best it will produce a better understanding of the doctrinal positions of divergent groups with a consequent change of attitude from one of mere toleration to one of appreciation and mutual respect. There is even less prospect of any kind of union among Christians, Jews, Moslems, Hindus, Buddhists, etc. But there undoubtedly will be a better mix of religious types in society. The urban milieu of the future will make Hindu and Shintoist the neighbors of Christians and Jews. From its current ecumenical posture, then, the theology of the future will have to assume one that is more transcendental. It will have to provide an understanding, hopefully with consequent appreciation and mutual respect, of less familiar forms of religion and the theologies associated with them. Even today Christians are exploring the meditation techniques of Zen. The future will, undoubtedly, open up more opportunities for contact with the result that every believer will become more conscious of and appreciative of the richness of his own religious heritage as well as of the elements that are common to it and other major religions. And theology in the future will serve to foster and explain that consciousness and appreciation.

The role of the priest today as well as in the past, and as it will be in the future, is unique. It is different from the role of the psychologist, the sociologist, the counselor, the politician, the humanitarian. The task of the priest is to be the official representative of the Church to his people. And the task of the Church today as always is to point to and objectify the sources of grace in the lives of its members and people in general. The priest as minister of the Church must bend every effort to make more conscious to men in his time the process of the gracing of mankind initiated in and by Jesus Christ and continued through the sacerdotal charism with which he endowed his Church. The tool that the priest uses to enhance this awareness is his professional knowledge, his theology. And the more suited this theology is to the task to be accomplished, the more satisfaction the priest will have as a professional man.

CHAPTER VI
The Priest as Apostle

Jesus himself could not have been looked upon as a priest by the people of his time. He was not of the tribe of Levi. He did not perform sacerdotal tasks in the Temple. The Gospel texts give us an account of his life and sayings. And, as we said, never once in the Gospel does he proclaim himself to be a priest. It was his followers, later on, after his death and resurrection, who after reflecting upon his claims and his deeds attributed a priestly role to him. It was a different kind of priesthood from that which Israel had known. It was priesthood New Testament style.

If Jesus did not call himself a priest, he did describe his role in life. He was a man with a task to perform. He was a man with a mission. And that mission was given him by the one who sent him. He had a message to deliver to the world from the one who sent him. And he had to authenticate that message, seal it with his own blood. Now the word "mission" is derived from a Latin term which best translates the Greek expression from which we get the word "apostle." An apostle is one sent by another with a job to do. He is an emissary. And the job he has to do is his mission.

The New Testament indicates that Christ was not an apostle in an ordinary sense. His special relationship to the one who sent him, the one he calls his Father, marks him out as unique among apostles or emissaries. True, like all apostles Jesus came to men with a message. He was the official representative of the Father who sent him. But since he was in nature identical with the Father, he brought with him more than just a message. He brought with him in his own being the originator and authenticator of that message. He brought with him in his divine nature the one who was identical with him in that nature. And even his own personality, though distinct from that of the Father, mirrors and images it. He is aptly described in early theology as the one and only sacrament of the Father. He renders truly present in himself the one whose apostle he is. "Philip, whoever sees me sees the Father" (John 14:9).

Because of the uniqueness of Christ's apostleship, the early Church apprehended him as an ideal mediator between God and man, a perfect *pontifex,* a priest. He alone among men could offer the perfectly acceptable sacrifice. And the sacrifice he did offer was doubly sanctified because it was the sacrifice of himself! The priestly charism of the Church partakes of the nature of the priesthood of Christ. Like Christ the Church too has a mission, an apostolate. And it is identical with Christ's. The persons whom the Church consecrates as priests in virtue of its sacerdotal charism can also be considered as apostles. In fact, the very essence of their priesthood, as we have seen, lies in their authorization to represent the Church. They are sent by the Church as Christ was sent by his Father. But since Christ has mystically identified himself with his Church, priests have been and can be aptly regarded as apostles of Christ. The priest represents Christ; he is a spokesman for Christ. In some measure he is invested with the authority and responsibility of Christ. He is empowered to some extent to make decisions in the name of Christ. He is a witness to Christ and the message Christ brought from his Father. The priest's very life is best seen as a charism testify-

ing to Christ. His very being and existence has to be the seal
that authenticates the words of Christ that are on his lips.

Thus Pope Pius XI in his encyclical letter on the priesthood states: "The priest is, as we are accustomed to say with
good reason, 'another Christ,' because in some way he represents the Person of Christ: 'As the Father has sent me, I also
send you.'" As Christ rendered his Father present in his own
person and being, so the priest brings with himself a presence
of Christ, particularly when he plays the role of Christ in his
sacramental ministrations. The document on the sacred liturgy of Vatican II acknowledges this fact when it speaks
about the various presences of Christ in the Church today. As
Christ was the image of the Father, so the priest is the image of
Christ. He is configured to Christ by the charism he receives
in the sacraments which brought him first to membership in
the priestly people and then to the ministry. Symbolically,
as we have seen, his identity with Christ is marked by the
anointings he receives. He becomes as a minister the living
sacrament of Christ as Christ was the sacrament of his Father. That is why the German theologian Karl Rahner can
define a priest simply as one who makes Christ present in
the world today.

But if the priest is another Christ, if he is an image of
Christ, if he is a representative of Christ, this is true because
he has Christ's job to do. He renders Christ present precisely
because he does Christ's work. In him mission is prior to
presence. If Christ was a priest of the new order because he
was the emissary, the apostle of his Father, sent into the
world to do the Father's thing, then the Catholic priest as
the emissary, the apostle of Christ, is sent into the world to do
Christ's thing. As an apostle like Christ, he has a mission,
an apostolate.

Rahner has defined that apostolate, as it appears concretely
in today's world, as the realization in the midst of a secular
situation of a Christian existence characterized by a marked

solicitude for the salvation of one's neighbor, and becoming by that very fact salvific. Vatican II considers every activity of the mystical body directed toward the goal that all men enter into a relationship with Christ and share in his saving redemptive act as part of the Church's apostolate. Consistent with our theology of priesthood, we would have to look upon the apostolate as the realization in our time of the paschal and pentecostal mysteries of Christ. The priest as apostle works and strives to actualize these two mysteries to the fullest extent possible. The paschal mystery, as we have said, is that which deals with guilt and sin. It is the mystery that promotes man's reconciliation with God, with himself and with his fellows. It is the mystery of justice and peace in society and among nations. The pentecostal mystery passes beyond peace and justice. It is the mystery of union and love. It is the mystery that promotes respect, mutual concern, true charity and love among men, unites them to one another and consequently brings them close to God.

Viewed as the realization in society of the Christian mysteries, the apostolate today does not further dichotomize the sacral and the secular. We have said that theology today is coming to appreciate more and more that Christ's redemptive act, while essentially concerned with the eternal salvation of man, includes also the renewal of the whole temporal order. The Church has always perceived the fact that the eternal and the temporal are inextricably linked in the Christian world view. So-called secular society also appreciates the values of reconciliation, justice and peace. Secular society also wishes to be rid of guilt and depravity. Secular society recognizes as ideal and aspires to a situation where men could live together in harmony and love. Yet these are the very values that Christianity views as conducive to eternal salvation. The goal of the Christian apostolate is not to subvert or change these aspirations of secular society, but merely to make that society conscious of the possibility of achieving them only in and through Christ. The apostle has to make the world aware of the graced condition that it is already in possession of through Christ, and to facilitate the commitment of men to the love of God proffered in grace, so that Christ's mysteries may be fully operative in them.

Closely allied to the issue of the sacral and the secular in the apostolate is the question of activity and passivity. The world achieves its goals by action. The world is Pelagian through and through. It believes that a man who just sits and waits, asks and hopes for some assistance from above and does not marshal his own resources is doomed to failure. The Church, on the other hand, casts a passive image of itself. It describes itself in terms of a following, not a leadership. It sees itself as principally being acted upon by God's grace, not as an initiator of action. The symbols of the Church that are traditional emphasize this passive, acolythatic self-concept: kingdom, sheepfold, temple of the presence, spouse, body (as opposed to head), people (as opposed to leader). Good Christians today identify with the role of sheep in the parable of the Good Shepherd. Yet the early Church evidently identified with Christ in his role of shepherd and projected non-believers as the sheep. For the early Church seemed to be much more conscious of its pastoral role than the Church today. Its job was to feed Christ in the person of others. As both Scripture and the liturgy intimate, Christ is both the shepherd and the lamb of God. In the believer it is the shepherd's role that has to be stressed; in the non-believer it is the lamb to be cared for and fed that is suggested by the image. While the apostolate has always been considered as activity on the part of that Church which casts such a passive image of itself, that activity has, understandably in the light of that image, been very limited and controlled. The specter of Pelagianism has always conjured up words of caution relative to the apostolate perceived as activity, and open condemnation of the "heresy of action" so dear to the secular American spirit.

It is true that even the apostolate itself, though the word is easily associated with action, has to be viewed in the first instance as a passive condition of members of the Church. If it is authentic, the essence of the apostolate consists in being sent by Christ to actualize his mysteries in society. Being sent, being given this mission, is the very essence of this task of the Church, because without this commission, it could not be designated as the work of Christ, as the continuation of his salvific action in our time. It is this characteristic of mission that marks the Christian apostolate as the highest form of communication possible between God and man. It is the sense of mission that gives the apostle his authority and makes him an authentic witness in the midst, perhaps, of a disbelieving world. It is this sense of mission that gives him hope. It is this sense of mission that assures success. But this whole question of mission-action involves a paradox. The mission is for action. One is not just sent; he is sent to do something. And relative to the Church's apostolate, the theological truth of the matter might well be that the mission is really identified with the action. It may be that the chief indicator of mission in a particular apostolic action is that action itself, not some decree or tradition. If any apostolic activity realizes in a particular situation the paschal and/or pentecostal mysteries, the sign of mission is already in evidence. It is only through God's activity that this could happen. The Gospel gives us the key. By their fruits we know them; apostolic activities are to be judged primarily by their results. That is the way the world judges success. And sometimes the children of the world are wiser in their generation than the children of light. There can be no results without trial. The world knows how to dare, to risk, to experiment, to test, to try. And the world knows how to recognize success. Because of Vatican II the Church too, fortunately, is now coming to realize that nothing

succeeds like success, especially when that success appears to
be God-given.

Paramount in the apostolate today is the question of varied
ministry. What seems to be called for is the widest possible
diversity of ministry and the most perfect possible singleness
of mission. To be sure, there is here a kind of mutual dependence. The more divergent the ministry, the more apparent will
become the oneness of mission. And conversely, the more
singular the mission, the wider will be the possibilities of its
application without being attenuated. The Church has in the
recent past felt so often that its apostolic objective would be
compromised unless its influence was restricted to the safer,
more traditional modes of operation. New ministries were re-
sisted. What experiments were actually tried, as the priest-
worker movement in France, failed. And failure, instead of
being accepted in a Christlike way, signaled the doom of future experiments. After Vatican II the prospects look better.
Today we see some attempts to set up team ministries, store-
front churches, exchange of pulpits and non-territorial parishes, among others. The multimedia approach of advertising
is influencing ministerial organization. As it is being incorpo-
rated more and more into liturgy and catechism, it is making
new demands upon apostles. It is, perhaps, calling for new
structural plans for the work of the apostolate. But the greater
the variation and diversification there is in the apostolate, and
the more this is tolerated and welcomed by the people of God,
the greater evidence there will be to the world of the presence
of the Spirit in the Church, that Spirit who alone can make
all things one.

Presupposing the power of God's presence, the apostle sets
out to extend that power and make it better felt in his milieu.
Like faith, as we have seen, the apostolate is founded equally
upon both the presence and the absence of God. It presupposes God's hiddenness as much as it presupposes his presence. If the Father himself had chosen to appear in the

world, Jesus could not have been his apostle. And if Jesus extended his visible presence to the world today in some universal manner priests would have no apostolate. As we have seen, the very notion of apostolate centers around a vicarious presence. God is rendered present through Jesus; and Jesus himself as well as his Father are rendered present to the world today through the Church and the apostles who represent it. As a matter of fact God characteristically has chosen to reveal himself to the masses of men through other men. And indeed since all men are images of God, in some sense God is present in all whether they recognize the fact or not. It is this recognition of the fact of God's presence in all that is the goal of the apostolate. For the apostolate is a ministry, the serving of God present in, imaged in, encoded in men. Luther realized this well when he called man the *larva Dei,* the mask of God. But because of God's formal absence, because of the absence of God in the world in the way man would expect him to appear, because the only presence of God in the world is a larval one, the work of the apostolate becomes a difficult one. It becomes a task primarily of witnessing God's presence in man in the paschal and pentecostal mysteries. And as we have stated in the chapter on faith, to witness, to testify today often means to take a risk, to expose oneself to loss, to appear foolish in the eyes of the world. It often means that one will have to live out the paschal and pentecostal mysteries, not just proclaim or celebrate them. It means that one may have to model these mysteries in his own life, so that the paradox of God's being will be more manifest to men. For to those who understand the meaning of Christ's mysteries, God's absence is really the sign of his presence; his silence is his spoken word; his restlessness is peace; his poverty enriches. He exercises mercy through judgment; he exalts by humiliating; he manifests his divinity through ministry.

If the apostolate of the Church is one of the manifestations of its priestly charism, a charism that is shared by clergy and laity, the emphasis that has been placed in recent times on lay apostolic involvement is indeed justified. Indeed to the extent that the clergy are considered a special class, separated from the world, different from ordinary people, they become less effective in modeling the Christian life in society. If they are stereotyped, if it is presumed that it is their job to preach Christ, then the witness they give may appear less authentic, less genuine, less spontaneous, less human. Thus some modern commentators on the effectiveness of the Church's mission in the modern world would lay the failure it has experienced, especially in Europe, where losses are greater than gains, to the mistake of not involving the laity in more responsible and extensive ways. Some writers voice the plea that Church authorities turn over the responsibility for the apostolate entirely to laymen. Others feel that the layman and not the priest is the one who must enter the lists of the apostolate, who must be active in promoting the faith, who must first confront non-believers with the issue of religion, and propose to them in word as well as action the values that Christianity can bring to their lives. The role of the priest in the operation would be that of a back-of-the-lines trainer and director. He would prepare the laymen so that they would feel and be adequate to their task. By his own life and witnessing of the Gospel values the priest would inspire the laymen to action. He would act as adviser and helper in time of difficulty. He would direct the strategy in general from his headquarters position, but the field direction would be in the hands of the laymen involved. The priest would provide for any resources laymen might need in carrying out their assignment. It would be the show of the lay priesthood. To be sure, the ministerial priest would still officially represent the Church in the operation. He would be the officer responsible. But his role would be more of a staff than field officer. He would work exclusively with the Catholic participants in the program. They in turn would contact the prospective converts. The priest would have to begin by convincing laymen of the truth inculcated by Vatican II: that they are the Church, that the responsibility for the growth of the Church does not rest exclusively with the clergy, that every Catholic has to be involved in fulfilling the command of Jesus to baptize all peoples, that the test of faith is not so much in receiving, but in the giving of oneself to help others to receive that gift which outstrips all others.

The style of priestly apostolic leadership implied in this view is perhaps one that would not appeal to very many priests. In the early Church certainly it was the priests who were first in the field. The great priestly heroes of those times when Christianity enjoyed its greatest triumph over paganism, and hundreds of thousands of people were converted to Christ, were no mere staff officers. They were deeply involved in the fray; the priests today want to be equally involved. But this perspective on the apostolate does contain the germ of a truth that must guide the Church's mission in the future. The work of the apostolate is not exclusively the preserve of ministerial priests; apostolic activity will be effective only inasmuch as the lay priesthood is spurred to action. And the work of the apostolate in the future will not be placed in the hands of individuals. It will be the responsibility of groups of priests and laymen working together, side by side, each entrusted with his own task in the total enterprise.

In such an apostolic group each member will be encouraged to develop and contribute his own abilities and skills to the project. Leadership roles will not automatically be awarded to the clergy, but will be shared, and undertaken by the one most qualified to handle each phase of the planned operation. Intercommunication among members will be fostered. Free discussion will be encouraged. Empathy and understanding will be emphasized. The group will analyze and

criticize its own functioning and its failure or success in attaining each objective it sets for itself; the advice of outside
experts will be solicited where necessary. High value will be
placed upon the openness of the group to assimilate new ideas,
to explore new methods and techniques, to tolerate and profit
from failure, to capitalize upon success. The ultimate effectiveness of the group will depend upon its ability to set up a
long-range goal, and short-range objectives leading to it, and
to progress continuously toward the final goal by taking objective after objective. Clear-sighted and realistic thinking and
planning in regard to both goal and objectives will be highly
prized by all in the group. A timetable will set a brisk pace
for the group in the achievement of its short-range objectives;
and a sensitivity to the emotional aura, psychic stamina and
physical energy of members of the group as well as an awareness of the time that can be devoted to this project, apart
from other work, will allow each participant to set his own
personal tempo, while not impeding the progress of the group
at large. As the group grows in its ability to integrate its
apostolic involvement with other aspects of the lives of its
members, it will begin to apprehend itself as a minimodel for
both the parish of which it is a part and for the Church itself.

Of course, such an idealized conception of an apostolic
group does not take into account the many difficult realities
that will be encountered in the formation of such a team.
There will be differences not only in semantics, in attitudes, in
theologies, in perspectives on life, but even in the perception
of the basic meaning and thrust of the Christian message itself. Here of course the leadership abilities of the priest will
be paramount. He must show himself not only to be well
enough versed in his own professional knowledge to smooth
out and effect an attitude of tolerance at first, and eventual
approval of theological differences, but also to be a student of
humanity skilled enough to cope with emotional conflict. He
will be able to point out to members of the group that they

all, no matter what their different personal views, have basically found in Christianity an answer to the deepest issue that every human being has to struggle with: the meaning of his own existence. And they have discovered answers to key questions related to this basic one: Is commitment possible? Is love worthwhile? Can society purge itself of evil? Is there a life after death? Does the individual have any dignity? The meaning and solace that they have found in the Christian answer to these fundamental questions about life is motive enough to spur them to overcome all obstacles in sharing their faith with others. But they often need the reassurance and help that only a priest, as official representative of the Church as well as a professional in his own field, can give.

If the first characteristic of the apostolate of the future is that it will be undertaken by groups of priests and laymen sharing responsibility and working together, the second is that it will revolve initially around the question of the meaning of human life. As we said, the new generation is much more tolerant of meaninglessness. In fact, in some quarters there seems to be a cult of the meaningfulness of meaninglessness. Satanic worship, black masses, witchcraft and voodoo are all indicators in our time that the absurd and evil still prey upon men's minds. But, as we also indicated, although the young person of today and the citizen of the future is much more comfortable than his elders with absurdity and meaninglessness and is prepared if necessary to live and cope with such conditions, withal there is still in evidence a basic search for meaning. The quest for an answer is carried on today as vigorously as it was in the past, less openly and flamboyantly perhaps, but nonetheless really. The young people today may not as yet have found an absolute to commit themselves to, but indications are that they are still looking for one.

Initiated with the question about the meaning of human life, then, the apostolate of the future will be loath to dichotomize religious and social issues for fear of once again raising the specter of the distinction between the sacral and the secular. The future apostle will simultaneously cultivate human and Christian values and will portray Christianity as a satisfying and potentially effective human response to the problems of the world. The divine elements in Christian teaching may for a while lie hidden like seeds in a pod, but in God's good time they will emerge, and only in God's good time, for he alone can give faith; the apostle can only open the minds and hearts of his contacts to truth, and so help them to be better disposed toward faith. The humanistic aspects of Christianity will be stressed, because if the social analysts of our day are correct, the whole youth culture that has been created in our time represents a powerful reaction to the loss of human values in our technocratic society. It is not only a countercultural but also a counterrevolutionary movement as it is described by these commentators. Some have compared it to the Luddite movement during the time of the industrial revolution. The technocratic revolution that makes its force felt everywhere today represents an invasion of human values. Ruthlessly it extends its tendrils into every nook and cranny of life. Young people oppose the white and unbloody but nonetheless real violence of this incursion. They are considered by analysts to be radical pacifists, neo-Luddites joining forces with other humanists in protesting the growing consciousness of their own imminent obsolescence. The humanistic breed is doomed to eventual extinction because they lack the salable skills, the hardness of character, the life-style and value patterns that are consonant with the new, emergent post-industrial society. So they carry on the fight as counterrevolutionaries against the inevitable evolution and spread of a new cybernetic consciousness in American society. They attack the symbols of this emergent consciousness, the computer, the research laboratory, the headquarters where is concentrated all of the numinosity of the military-industrial cartel that fosters the revolution. Like the Luddites, in protest they assume in their personal appearance and life-style the symbols of a former, in this case, the pioneer period of American history, when human values counted and rugged individualism was the law of the land.

Prognosticators warn that this counterrevolution carried on by the youth of our time is bound to fail. It will be crushed by the technocratic juggernaut just as the Luddites were beaten down by the success of the industrial revolution.

Students of the counterrevolution warn that it should not be regarded simply as a revolt against reason. The movie *If . . .* portrays the headmaster of a British school as pleading with his rioting charges to be reasonable. As he cries out: "Let's reason about this!" he is shot in the head. But the youth culture opposes only that caricature of reason that reminds them of the inhuman logic of the computer. They are not against reason itself, but only against a use of logic to bypass or ignore human values, feelings and needs.

The apostle of the future, then, in his support of human values, will like Christ himself, if the social prophets are correct, be fighting a losing battle. He will have to espouse a cause that is doomed to failure. His role will be to give comfort and support to those who are losing with him in their hour of need, and to hold forth to them the promise of a resurrection, a way out, in the future. And he will wisely employ logic and reason to enhance other human values. The theology that he will use, though based upon science, will be eminently experiential, and so will take due account of human feeling, emotion, awareness and desire. The apostle of the future will point out to the world of his time the value of being human as surely as Christ through his sufferings and death did for his.

The apostle of the future will have to cultivate in his own personal life some of the virtues prized by the counterrevolutionary humanistic society he will serve. He will have to manifest a certain air of freedom from the strictures and imperatives of the establishment. He will have to cultivate absolute honesty and openness. He will have to avoid secretiveness of all kinds. He will have to project a certain wholesomeness about himself. He will have to have attained a certain measure of self-fulfillment. He will be an opponent of role-playing and manipulation. He will be genuine in his own feelings and in the manifestation of them to others. He will strive as far as possible to maintain a non-judgmental position with regard to the personal habits and life-style of others, though he will have to take a strong position on such social issues as the war, race, ecology, etc. He will manifest himself and encourage among his acquaintances a spirit of non-competitiveness. He will have to be the exact antithesis of the proper and efficient businessman. He will have to be conscious of the goals and objectives of the community of which he is a member. And he will have to promote them even at the cost of personal sacrifice. He will not pretend to offer a complete blueprint for the future, but will strive only to inculcate some meaningfulness in humanistic terms for life as it is currently being lived.

If the man of the future like modern man will feel lonely, isolated, insignificant, faceless, then the focus off the personal and onto the group that the apostle experiences in his own training and operation will be of help to those whom he serves too. He will show them how to achieve friendship despite personal defects. Being conscious himself of the great trust placed in him by the apostolic group, he will try to communicate the experience of his own self-worth that he has had to others by in turn trusting them. He will try to stimulate and excite a new group consciousness among those with whom he is working so that they might enjoy the same benefits as he does from his association with the other members of his apostolic team. He will try to arouse in these groups the same aspirations he once experienced and felt to be fulfilled

through his Christian commitment: true freedom; respect for
the uniqueness of the individual; meaningful dialogue; reconciliation with and understanding of one's neighbor; charity and
peace; a view of life to live by. By the impact of his own life he
will set as their goal the humanization of societal structures to
the extent possible in the circumstances. And he will proclaim
that this was the essential task of Jesus, and that the values to
which they aspire are the ones that Jesus can impart.

And the apostle of the future will point out to the people
whom he serves the principles by which the technocratic,
business-dominated world of the future may well come to
live. They are principles proposed by the Italian savant Niccolò Machiavelli in the sixteenth century: The acquisition
of wealth is the supreme value in human life; it is the duty of
public authority to facilitate the prosperity of the clever and
intelligent. Self-interest is the most basic human trait; every
man has his price. Fear is the most reliable motive force; men
will do anything to escape threat to their well-being. The
masses of people are patently stupid, believing in anything,
and weak, ready to be swayed by a show of strength; the
crafty and strong man should be confident of success in any
project, if only it is clever and moving. There is a constant
craving among the masses of people for new pleasures and
gratifications; the person who can use this craving to manipu-
late them to do his bidding will rise to the top. But the future apostle will also demonstrate that these principles are
diametrically opposed to those of Jesus Christ and his followers, who seek to reconcile men to live together in mutual
respect, peace and justice. He will explain to them and model
for them the meaning of Christian love, the love of God himself that he has deigned to share with men.

But the ultimate test of apostleship in the future, as well
as now and in the past, will be the ability to put oneself in the
place of the persons whom one is sent to serve. The one who

is able to identify with, empathize with, feel for and introject his apostolic clientele will be the perfect and most effective apostle. For he will be like Christ himself, who, being God, was able to put himself perfectly in our place.

CHAPTER VII
The Priest as Mystagogue

In the chapter on the professional knowledge of the priest we pointed out that the theology of the past was mystadelic; that is, it tended to dispel the mysteries of religion by attempting to make them seem more reasonable, if not to explain them. On the contrary, we said, the theology of the future, if we can prognosticate from current trends, will be mystagogic; that is, it will lead men to mystery; it will tend to build up mystery, support it, make it more awesome and impressive. If this is true, the priest will appear more and more as the man of mystery, the keeper of the secrets, the guardian of the occult, the initiator into the mystic, the mystagogue. We indicated in the last chapter that the youth culture of our time in reaction against the cybernetic revolution is highly suspicious of cultivated logic, rationality and universal principles, the essential ingredients of any traditional philosophical system. It expresses instead a mounting interest in the alogical but experience-related transcendental. It delves down not only into the depths of the human psyche but also into the reaches of the drug-induced fantasy to find a symbolism that will blow the mind, that will be truly psychedelic. Its religious feelings find an outlet in astrology, oriental mysticism, occultism and even witchcraft and satanism. Ancient and esoteric ethnic cults like Jewish cabalism and Celtic druidism are becoming increasingly more popular. And from the satanist's pentagram attention is turning also to the alchemist's formula and the old-time magician's handbook. Already there is manifested great interest in the *Corpus Hermeticum* that dominated Renaissance magic from the fifteenth to the seventeenth centuries. It was one of the chief sources employed by occultists like Marsilio Ficino, Pico della Mirandola, Henry Agrippa, Giordano Bruno and Tommaso Campanella in their attempt to reconcile theology and magic. The current interest may well presage a desire in certain sectors of the youth culture to achieve a kind of synthesis between occult science and Christian principles.

Hermetism is explored thoroughly in A. J. Festugière's *La révélation d'Hermès Trismégiste* published in four volumes at Paris from 1950 to 1954. This thorough study reveals Hermetism as it appeared in Renaissance times as a recrudescence of an ancient Gnostic doctrine with which St. Augustine and other Fathers of the Church were well acquainted. Hermetism basically is an attempt to amalgamate magic and Christian truth. It proposes the idea that the Christian revelation was anticipated in the writings of an ancient Egyptian seer, Hermes Trismegistus. Some identified Hermes with Thoth, the ibis-headed secretary god in the Egyptian pantheon, and his counterparts Hermes in the Greek and Mercury in the Roman religious cult. Others consider him to be just a human magician who knew the secrets of nature and of the gods. In 1471 Ficino finished and published a new Latin translation of the *Pimander,* the first book of the Hermetic scriptures. It created quite a stir among theologians, who immediately perceived its similarity to both the book of Genesis and the Christian mysteries. Many tried to interpret the divine *Nous* of *Pimander* in a Christian sense as alluding to the divine word, the second Person of the Trinity. But it was the first human being in *Pimander* who, like the Adam of Genesis, reveals the basis for all occultism, magic and mystery. He desires to know all things. Good or evil: he wants to assimilate everything and so be in control of all things. Here we encounter again a kind of all-pervasive idea in ancient literature, the idea that knowledge is power. For the first man of *Pimander* wants also the power to create. He wants to be like God. And the key to divine power is knowledge of all things.

The story in Genesis about Adam's naming of the beasts has always had great significance for both Jewish and Christian theology. In naming the beasts Adam comes to know them. But in the theology of the ancients knowledge is related to creation. To know a thing means to bring it into existence as far as the knower is concerned. This is how man is portrayed as a creator in *Pimander* too. His ability to identify reality and impart some significance to it for himself is considered as a truly creative power. Knowledge is a new kind of creation, a re-creation for man of the reality brought into being by God. That reality is brought into significant existence for man through his experience of it. The idea that knowing is equivalent to creating is also expressed in the fact that in some ancient languages the verb "to know" is also employed in the sense of "to have fruitful intercourse with." Thus Eve brings forth a son as the result of Adam's "knowledge" of her.

Perhaps this view also extended beyond the Middle East in ancient times. Classicists are acquainted with a legend about the city of Rome. The Eternal City is said to have had, besides the name "Rome" which was known to people at large, a secret name known only to the emperors and priests. This name was guarded jealously because of the same notion that knowing the real name of anything gives the knower power over it. Only those public officials who were dedicated to the preservation of the Roman way of life and held power in virtue of their office were entitled to know the secret name. In later times it was especially feared that the secret might fall

into the hands of the barbarians and enable them to subvert
and capture the city.

What was the secret name of Rome? By now the careful
reader will want to know the answer to this question. His interest has perhaps been piqued. He wants to penetrate the secret, to solve the mystery, to know and so to have some kind
of power. He is experiencing himself the principle upon
which *Pimander* and the mystery cults of ancient times are
based. Man desires to know all things. When he is led to
mystery, he wants to involve himself in it, to experience the
challenge of it and to produce some satisfactory solution of it,
at least for himself, so that it will have some significance for
him, and he will have at least some power over it.

The Latin name of the Eternal City was *Roma*. The secret
name was said to be that word spelled backward: *Amor,* the
Latin word for love.

The revelation of the secret places the *cognoscenti* in a
privileged position. They know. They are set apart, in a caste
by themselves. They can use their knowledge. They can make
others who will become interested in the issue, in the mystery,
dependent upon them. Their knowledge gives them power not
only over what they know, but also to a certain extent over the
people who seek to know what they know. They have automatically achieved a kind of technological leadership in society.

In the medieval world too there are evidences of the viabil-
ity of this belief that knowledge is power not only among the
occultists but in Catholic orthopraxy as well. One instance
would be the ritual of exorcism. One of the steps in the process of driving a devil out of a possessed person is devoted to
the ascertainment of the name of the devil or devils involved.
Great importance is attached to the success of this stratagem.
The evil spirit is adjured in the name of God and of Jesus to
reveal his secret. The implication is that once the exorcist has

discovered the name proper to the troublesome demon he will have power over him.

In our own day some commentators have viewed the phenomenon of protest as a manifestation of the same belief. To protest against an evil is to believe that it can be destroyed by naming it. To denounce an abuse when the whole world is watching on television, even though the denunciation is only printed on a sign, is to make great numbers of people aware of it, and so, presumably, to deprive it of its power to influence.

In *Pimander* the first man, as the prototype of all men, like the Adam of Genesis wants to know all things, good and evil, and so be like God, having power over all. But there is a great divergence in the way this desire is evaluated in Genesis and *Pimander*. In Genesis it is obviously evil, the root of all sin, the sin of sins, that man should want to be like God, knowing all things; that he is not satisfied with just being man, limited in his knowledge and power. In *Pimander*, on the other hand, it is seen as something good and beautiful and constructive in man. It is man's greatest boast. It is his true excellence that he wants to know all things. It is the way to his attainment of power over all things and to complete self-fulfillment and happiness. For this reason Hermes Trismegistus emerges for cultivators of the Renaissance spirit as the *priscus theologus*, spokesman for the humanistic movement.

In this notion of the equivalence of knowledge and power we have the Hermetic explanation of the origin of man's interest in the mysterious and the occult. No man knows until he has himself penetrated the secret, until he has solved or at least experienced it, what power it contains. Man is moved by an inexorable drive to know as much as he can, and at least to experience by acting out what he cannot understand. What is hidden, what is mysterious, what is secret is precisely what is enticing and intriguing because it triggers that drive. It presents a challenge. It tempts man's creative power.

The Hermetic scriptures offer man a gnosis, secret information that can make him master both of himself and of the universe. Catholic philosophers like Marsilio Ficino and Pico della Mirandola, working under constant surveillance by the Inquisition, were generally clever enough to defend in them a value that was consonant with the dogmatic understandings of the times. They expounded a "natural magic," that is, a mastery of creation achieved through the understanding of the real nature of things, and the discovery of the hidden links and covert mutual influences that exist among all creatures. Occultism, witchcraft and black magic were to all appearances rejected as the operation of the devil, though it is obvious that these writers were also deeply affected by such practices. Some, like Giordano Bruno and Tommaso Campanella, were not always able to maintain the distinction and fell victim to the inquisitorial process.

The book on occult philosophy published by Henry Cornelius Agrippa represents a typical survey of the Hermetic view of creation and indicates the possibilities of its integration with Christian doctrine. The three parts deal respectively with natural magic or that emanating from the physical constitution of the universe, celestial magic or the connection between basic Christian doctrines like the Trinity and redemptive incarnation on the one hand, and zodiacal and astrological images on the other; and finally ritual or ceremonial magic, or that pursuant to man's desire to conciliate, to honor and worship transcendent power.

The point that medieval and Renaissance books on magic, like that of Cornelius Agrippa, make, issued as they were under the hawkish scrutiny of officers of the Inquisition, is one that is important for the mystagogue of our time. Human beings are forever interested in the occult, in mystery, in the transcendent. But Christianity is the guardian of the divine mysteries, mysteries so deep, so secret, so transcendent that they remain forever a challenge to the human mind. And yet to know them, to experience them not only provides life with a meaning, but also gives man a certain power over God himself, for God has promised to let his creative influence operate in the sacramentalization and acting out of those mysteries. Christianity is really a religion of mystery, more than all the ancient mystery cults. But its mysteries are both akin to and deeper than those that formed the bases of pagan religious and magical rituals.

Christianity does unfold in an eminent way the magic with which Cornelius Agrippa was concerned. It deals with natural magic and provides a stable view of the meaning of life and of the universe itself, one that can transform man into a responsible creature cognizant of his authentic role in the world. It primarily regards the celestial magic whereby God became man to intertwine and interlace forever human and divine identity and destiny. And it provides ritual magic, a magic that renders God himself present in a loving and transforming way to those who dedicate themselves to him by acting out his mysteries.

The mysteries of Christianity are to the believer the really authentic mysteries. Belief in them leads to true and worthwhile power. It leads to the power that is God's very own. It enables men to love God and their fellow men as God himself does.

But it is not sufficient for the Christian mystagogue merely to know those mysteries, or even just to experience them operative in his own life. If he is to preside over them, if he is to lead others to them, he must know the techniques of the mystagogue. He must learn the art of enveloping men in mystery, of piquing their interest, of opening up to them the dark recesses of their own being, of capturing for them in image and symbol the sublime truths of their religious belief. And this is an art he can best learn by acquainting himself with the methods and techniques of the mystery religions of past eras, seeing that the mystadelic penchant of Christian theology has

robbed him of any significant native heritage in this regard.
Before the recent liturgical reform the ritual itself provided a
certain mysterious aura for the priest. The ceremonial language was Latin. The meaning of copious gestures was often
not fully understood even by the priest. The altar was so situated as to protect the secret. The priest robed in mystic ves-
ture was the chief actor; the people merely knelt and watched
in awesome silence. But now that all of this is gone, the priest
will no longer be automatically constituted, but will have to
learn how to be, a mystagogue.

Philologists opine that the word "mystery" is derived from
the Greek verb *muein,* which means "to close." And researchers
on the ancient mystery religion inform us that in context it
meant to close the mouth and/or the eyes. The truths dealt
with were *arrēta,* unspeakable, incommunicable, not fully
understandable. But by that very fact they demanded a kind
of blind faith, a trust in the one who cultivated and performed
them, as well as in the one who revealed them. The mystagogue inculcated a sense of awe more by keeping silence
than by speaking. He kept his mouth shut. He let the ritual
speak. He inculcated in his followers the trait of not turning to
him for answers, but of looking inward in silence to the hidden recesses of their own being. He taught more by implication, symbol and parable than by direct communication. But
most importantly of all, he knew how to close his own eyes as
well as his mouth. He fully believed and trusted in the numen
he possessed. He appreciated the fact that he himself must be
led to mystery by it and by it alone. As his followers were led
by him, he had to allow himself to be directed by it. He was
enthused by it. He was possessed by it. He constantly turned
to it. It was the charism of his leadership of others.

The mystagogue realizes that the earth is shrouded in mystery. It is the enigma whence all mystery emanates. It reveals
in itself the paradox of growth. Its relationship with the sun
deciphers for man the rhythm of birth and death of its vege-

tation, that vegetation upon which all land-bound life ultimately feeds. The renovation of nature in the spring, the
birth that heralds the renewal of the growth process, is celebrated with mask and paint that imitates the seed hiding the
new life of the grain in it; it is expressed in dance that acceler-
ates the measured, agonizing rhythm of nature's eternal self-
renewal, with song and shouting and prayer to hasten the
process of the renewal of the face of the earth, to render the
barren fields green with life. The Eleusinian mystagogue
raises his eyes to heaven and cries: *"Hue!"* (rain), and then
gazes at the earth and shouts: *"Kue!"* (conceive). He celebrates the mystery of birth and death, of fertility and growth,
of natural elements that have become ultimates in human
life. And as the seeds are planted in the ground, the process is
symbolized by sexual involvement. The most radical concerns
of man are the preservation of the race and the feeding of it.
All life is impelled by these two natural thrusts, but in humanity they achieve the status of a pastoral concern. The mystery of the earth reaches its highest and most sublime expression in man.

The mystagogue points to the goal of involvement. It is
ecstasy. It is being rapt out of oneself by the object one wor-
ships. It is transcendence. It is escape from earth by identification with its mystery. It is being possessed by the power
that moves the earth and the heavens. It is becoming a catechumen, a *katexomenos,* a possessed one.

The initial step to the goal is indicated by the mystagogue.
It is purification. The initiate must abstain from what would
impede the attainment of ecstasy (*agneia*). But he must also
positively purge himself of evil and render himself ritually
pure in the sacred bath or holy fire (*katharmos*). Only then
can he sit at the common meal with his fellow initiates and
experience acceptance into the brotherhood. Only then does
he receive the secret knowledge that will give him true power.
Only then is the very heart and essence of the mystery com-

municated to him (*paradosis*). Only then does he become an authentic celebrant of the mystery (*mustēs*). But ritual purity is required not so much for the revelation of the secret, for the uncovering of the sacred symbols, for participation in the common meal of the brotherhood, for full acceptance into the cult as for the personal action of the initiated. For the mystery itself centers in the personal action of the cultist, in his behavior, in his reaction to the milieu of life in which he finds himself situated. To highlight this fact the mystagogue will often cause the message of the mystery, indeed, the mystery itself if that is possible, to be re-enacted, to be presented in dramatic form, so that the initiate will have a model for his own action. In this way the mystery will be memorialized for the cultist (*mimnēsis*), and he will more easily become an imitator of it in his life (*mimos*). So the mystery itself through the activity of the mystagogue is oriented toward future action, rooted in the memory of the legendary past, and symbolized in the present.

But by far the most important and most difficult task of the mystagogue is to relate the mystery to the lives of the initiated. To really grasp, to really possess the mystery that is revealed and celebrated, the initiate must closely link it with the mystery of life. In the past man has been intrigued by the basically unfathomable process of birth, growth and death, and by the inexplicable interplay of good and evil in his existence. Today he may well be more puzzled by the mystery of his identity and his role in the world as well as his responsibility for the future. This too is fundamentally a mystery of earth, which, illumined by the revelation Christ has made, lends itself to the art of the mystagogue.

Apart from his skill in working with mystery, certain personal traits will be highly valued in the mystagogue of tomorrow's Church. Most prized will be his integrity of life: the sincerity of his own belief in the mystery and dedication to it, and the attainment of an authentic identity and personal satisfaction and fulfillment through it. He will be effective as a mystagogue to the extent that he himself is possessed by the mystery. He must demonstrate himself to be enthusiastic for and fully loyal to the mystery. He will be respectful of the mystery of personality in each individual he serves; he will acknowledge, respect and honor the uniqueness of each while also being sensitive to the needs and goals of the society in which he labors. He will know how to conciliate in conflict, to be permissive with those who are sorely tried, to be enigmatic with the wise, to be empathic with the humble, resourceful with those seeking to dedicate themselves to the mystery. He will run the risk of trusting. His goal will be growth to the point of ecstasy. His measuring stick of success will be love. His mien will be open and free, but he will not deviate from the demands of the mystery. He will devote himself regularly to introspection and meditation. He will be a true cultivator of the spirit. His presence will always reflect the awe, the wonder, the respect he has for the mystery.

The priest of the future should have no reason at all to feel uncomfortable in his role as mystagogue. True, the Church of the recent past did not exploit the potentialities of the ineffable mysteries that lie at the very center of its being and form the heart of its life. But the early Church was very much aware of its relationship to the mysterious. It was too close to the Gospel itself to be oblivious of it. Early Christians could hardly forget the words of Jesus himself in the Gospel of Mark that "the mystery of the kingdom of God" had been entrusted to their safekeeping (*to mustērion . . . tēs basileias tou theou*, 4:11). They were well acquainted with St. Paul's frequent reference to the mystery of Christianity. They knew how he spoke of the "mystery of the Good News" (Eph. 6:19). They remembered how he suffered, how he wound up in chains for faithfully proclaiming "the mystery of Christ" (Col. 4:3). The early Church was especially cognizant of Paul's own identification of Christ as the "mystery of God . . .

in whom are hidden away all the treasures of wisdom and knowledge" (Col. 2:2–3). Nor could the real meaning of Paul, the mystagogue, have escaped the people of this time when he referred to the mystery of sex and marriage as an analogue of the mystery of the union that exists between Christ and his Church (Eph. 5:32). But most especially were those who felt called by God to carry on the missionary work of evangelizing initiated by Paul and others familiar with his injunction that all regard men like Apollo and Cephas and himself as "stewards of the mysteries of God" (1 Cor. 4:1).

It is this stewardship of mystery, of the deep and unfathomable mystery of God that is Christ with all the richness of his wisdom and knowledge as well as the awesome power that flows from it, that will challenge the priest of the future to a life that will be fascinating, rewarding and fulfilling. It will be the celebration, inculcation and living of the paschal and pentecostal mysteries, constitutive, as we have said, of the very essence of the sacerdotal charism he possesses as a minister, as an ambassador, as a representative of the Church, that will spur the priest of the future on to fulfill faithfully and well his role as a mystagogue. For in the future it will be that role especially that will single him out from men of every other profession and mark him as a man of God, another Christ and worthy minister of his Church.

Bibliography

Significant Books

Bastian, R. J. *Priesthood and Ministry*. N.Y., Paulist Press, 1969.

Baum, W. *Considerations Towards a Theology of the Presbyterate*. Toledo, Ohio, West & Midward, 1961.

Blomjous, J. J. *Priesthood in Crisis*. Milwaukee, Bruce, 1969.

Bouëssé, H. *L'Évêque dans l'église du Christ*. Bruges, Desclée de Brouwer, 1963.

———— *Le Sacerdoce chrétien*. Bruges, Desclée de Brouwer, 1957.

Boulet, R. *The Sacramental Grace of the Priesthood*. Montreal, Université de Montréal, 1964.

Bouyer, L. *Le Sens de la vie sacerdotale*. Tournai, Desclée, 1960.

Brown, R. *Priest and Bishop: Biblical Reflections*. Paramus, N.J., Paulist, 1970.

Bunnik, R. J. *Priests for Tomorrow*. N.Y., Holt, Rinehart & Winston, 1969.

Carré, A.-M. *Le Vrai Visage du prêtre*. Paris, Cerf, 1959.

Charue, A. *Le Clergé diocésain*. 2. éd. Bruges, Desclée, 1960.

Cleary, W. *Hyphenated Priests: the Ministry of the Future*. N.Y., Corpus Books, 1969.

Colson, J. *L'Épiscopat catholique*. Paris, Cerf, 1963.

———— *L'Évêque dans les communautés primitives* . . . Paris, Cerf, 1951.

————*La Fonction diaconale aux origines de l'église*. Brussels, Desclée de Brouwer, c. 1960.

———— *Ministre de Jesus-Christ, ou le sacerdoce de l'évangile*. Paris, Beauchesne, 1965.

Congar, Y. *A Gospel Priesthood*. N.Y., Herder & Herder, 1967.

Denis, H. *Le Prêtre de demain*. Paris-Tournai, Casterman, 1967.

Dillenschneider, C. *Le Christ, l'unique prètre et nous ses prêtres*. Paris, Éditions Alsatia, 1960.

Doronzo, E. *Tractatus dogmaticus de ordine*. v. 1. Milwaukee, Bruce, 1957.

Duquesne, J. *A Church Without Priests?* N.Y., Macmillan, 1969.

Enciclopedia del sacerdozio. Firenze, Libreria editrice fiorentina, 1953.

Études sur le sacrement de l'ordre. Paris, Cerf, 1957.

Fourrey, R. *La Tradition sacerdotale*. Le Puy, Éditions X. Mappus, 1959.

Galot, J. *Visage nouveau du prêtre*. Gembloux, Duculot, 1970.

Greeley, A. M. *New Horizons for the Priesthood*. N.Y., Sheed & Ward, 1970.

———— *Priests for Tomorrow*. Notre Dame, Ind., Ave Maria, 1964.

———— *Priests in the United States: Reflections on a Survey*. Garden City, N.Y., Doubleday, 1972.

———— *Uncertain Trumpet: the Priest in Modern America*. N.Y., Sheed & Ward, 1968.

Gryson, R. *Le Ministère des femmes dans l'Église ancienne*. Gembloux, Duculot, 1972.

Guerry, E. *L'Évêque*. Paris, Fayard, 1954.

Hughes, J. *Man for Others: Reflections on the Christian Priesthood*. London, Sheed & Ward, 1971.

Instituto "Juan de Avila," Burgos, Spain. *Teología del sacerdocio*. Burgos, Ediciones Aldecoa, 1969.

Johannes, F. V. *Rethinking the Priesthood*. London, Gill & Macmillan, 1970.

Kempf, P., comp. *The Authentic Image of the Priest*. St. Meinrad, Ind., Abbey Press, 1970.

Klein, W. *A Priest Forever*. New York, Morehouse, 1964.

162   BIBLIOGRAPHY

Küng, H. *Why Priests?* Garden City, N.Y., Doubleday, 1972.

Laplace J. *Le Prêtre à la recherche de lui-même.* Paris, Éditions du Chalet, 1969.

Leclercq, J. *Man of God for Others.* Westminster, Md., Newman, 1968.

Lécuyer, J. *Le Sacerdoce dans le mystère du Christ.* Paris, Cerf, 1957.

Leplay, M. *Prêtres et pasteurs.* Paris, Mame, 1968.

Magner, J. *The Catholic Priest in the Modern World.* Milwaukee, Bruce, 1957.

Marchand, J.-P. *Prêtre, demain? Une question pour tout jeune chrétien.* Paris, Éditions Fleurus, 1967.

Masure, E. *Parish Priest.* Chicago, Fides, 1953.

Mohler, J. A. *The Origin and Evolution of the Priesthood; a Return to the Sources.* N.Y., Alba House, 1970.

Nash, N., and Rhymer, J. *The Christian Priesthood.* London, Darton, Longman & Todd, 1970.

Nouwen, H. J. M. *Creative Ministry.* Garden City, N.Y., Doubleday, 1971.

———— *Wounded Healer: Ministry in Contemporary Society.* Garden City, N.Y., Doubleday, 1972.

Nugent, F., comp. *The Priest in Our Day.* Westminster, Md., Newman, 1954.

O'Neill, D. *The Priest in Crisis: a Study in Role Change.* Dayton, O., Pflaum, 1968.

Passman, B., ed. *The Experience of Priesthood.* London, Darton, Longman & Todd, 1968.

Pellegrino, M. *The True Priest: the Priesthood as Preached and Practiced by St. Augustine.* N.Y., Philosophical Library, 1968.

Perrin, J. *The Minister of Christ.* Dubuque, Iowa, Priory Press, 1964.

Pflieger, M. *Priestly Existence.* Westminster, Md., Newman, 1957.

Power, D. *Ministers of Christ and His Church.* London, G. Chapman, 1969.

Prêtres d'hier et d'aujourd'hui. Paris, Cerf, 1954.

The Priest of the People: a Symposium. Westminster, Md., Newman, 1956.

Protat, J. *Le Clergé diocésain* . . . 2. éd. Bruges, Desclée de Brouwer, 1960.

Rahner, K., ed. *The Identity of the Priest.* N.Y., Paulist Press, 1969.

Rétif, A. *Le Prêtre et la mission.* Paris, Éditions Alsatia, 1964.

Salaun, R. *Qu'est-ce qu'un prêtre?* Paris, Éditions du Seuil, 1966.

Schlelke, K. *Discipleship and Priesthood.* N.Y., Herder & Herder, 1965.

Secondo, L. *The Twentieth Century Popes and the Priesthood.* Rome, Catholic Book Agency, 1957.

Senger, B. *Die priesterlichen Dienstämter und der Ordensstand: nach den Aussagen des 2. Vatikanischen Konzils.* Dülmen, Laumann, 1967.

Simonet, A. *The Priest and His Bishop.* St. Louis, B. Herder, 1969.

Sloyan, G., ed. *The Secular Priest in the New Church.* N.Y., Herder & Herder, 1967.

Thils, G. *Nature et spiritualité du clergé diocésain.* 2. éd. Bruges, Desclée de Brouwer, 1948.

Trapè, A. *Il sacerdote, uomo di Dio e servo della Chiesa.* Milano. Ancora, 1968.

Van Zeller, H. *The Gospel Priesthood,* N.Y., Sheed & Ward, 1956.

Veuillot, P., ed. *The Catholic Priesthood According to the Teaching of the Church.* 2 v. Westminster, Md., Newman, 1958–64.

Weitzel, E., ed. *Pastoral Ministry in a Time of Change.* Milwaukee, Bruce, 1966.

Current Articles

Ancel, A. "Le Sacerdoce ministériel." *Documentation catholique,* 67:622–29 (July 5, 1970).

Armbruster, C. "Ministry in Future Shock." *Chicago Studies,* 10:134–53 (Summer, 1971).

Begley, J. "The Office and Ministry of Priests: New Approaches." *American Ecclesiastical Review,* 165:84–92 (October, 1971).

Bertrand, J. "The Priest of Being." *Chicago Studies,* 5:239–51 (Fall, 1966).

Blenkinsopp, J. "Presbyter to Priest: Ministry in the Early Church." *Worship,* 41:428–38 (August–September, 1967).

Campbell, J. "Priestly Identity, Role and Function." *Priest,* 26:27–32 (December, 1970); 27:25–34 (February, 1971).
"Priests in Trouble." *Priest,* 27:17–21 (May, 1971).

Carr, A. "Priesthood=X?" *Priest,* 27:9–16 (January, 1971).

Caster, M. van. "The Priest in the Midst of Present Changes." *Lumen Vitae,* 25:461–82 (September, 1970).

Cleary, R. "Presbyterate in the Early Church." *Priest,* 26:6–19 (May, 1970).

Congar, Y. "Quelques problèmes touchant les ministères." *Nouvelle revue théologique,* 93:785–800 (December, 1971).

"Consensus on Ministry: Pluralism and Service." *National Catholic Reporter,* 7:1 (August 27, 1971).

Coppens, J. "Le Sacerdoce chrétien." *Nouvelle revue théologique,* 92:224–45 (March, 1970); 337–64 (April, 1970).

Crehan, J. "Ministerial Priesthood: a survey of Work Since the Council." *Theological Studies,* 32:489–99 (September, 1971).

Culligan, K. "Man's Religious Needs: Basis of a Relevant Priesthood." *Spiritual Life,* 17:105–12 (Summer, 1971).

Daniélou, J. "Des prêtres passionés de Dieu et passionés des hommes." *Documentation catholique,* 67:978–81 (November 1, 1970).
"The Universal Priesthood and the Ministerial Priesthood." *Osservatore Romano* (English), 24:168 (June 17, 1971).

Digan, P. "The Four Futures of Priesthood." *Furrow,* 22:535–46 (September, 1971).

Dodd, W. "Toward a Theology of the Priesthood." *Theological Studies,* 28:683–705 (December, 1967).

Donovan, D. "Toward a Theology of the Ministry." *Homiletic & Pastoral Review,* 70:489–99 (April, 1970).

Dries, A. "Priestly Roles and Personal Satisfaction." *Priest,* 27:45–50 (September, 1971).

Durrwell, F. "The Priest in the Church." *Lumen Vitae,* 24:297–333 (June, 1969).

Echlin, E. "The Once and Future Priesthood." *Review for Religious,* 28:235–43 (March, 1969).

Futrell, J. "What Is the Priesthood?" *Priest,* 27:17–26 (April, 1971).

Gaboury, P. "Prêtre: pasteur ou professionel?" *Revue de l'Université d'Ottawa,* 39:228–48 (April–June, 1969).

Galot, J. "L'accesso della donna ai ministeri della Chiesa," *La civiltà cattolica,* 123:317–29 (n. 2926, 20 maggio 1972).

"Les Caractère sacerdotal selon le Concile de Trente." *Nouvelle revue théologique,* 93:923–46 (November, 1971).

"The Priesthood of Consecrated Persons." *Review for Religious,* 31:178–86 (March, 1972).

Garrigues, J.-M., Le Guillou, M.-J., and Riou, A. "Le Caractère sacerdotal dans la tradition des Pères grecs." *Nouvelle revue théologique,* 93:801–20 (October, 1971).

Glaser, J. "Anonymous Priesthood." *Commonweal,* 93:271–74 (December 11, 1970).

Haslinger, J. "Priestly Expectations." *Priest,* 27:74–80 (October, 1971).

Hassel, D. "The Priest-Expert: a Philosophical-Theological Assessment." *Chicago Studies,* 3:201–25 (Fall, 1964).

Horvath, T. "Theology of a New Diaconate." *Revue de l'Université d'Ottawa,* 38:248–76 (April–June, 1968); 495–523 (July–September, 1968).

Hughes, J. "Man for Others . . . Man for God." *Priest,* 26:7–16 (December, 1970).

Kiesling, C. "Theology of the Priesthood for the Seventies." *Cross & Crown,* 24:19–27 (March, 1972).

Kollar, N. "Old and New in Theology of the Priesthood." *American Ecclesiastical Review,* 164:145–53 (March, 1971).

Koval, J., and Mills, E. "Stress in the Ministry." *IDOC,* 33:3–13 (October 16, 1971).

Lawler, J. G. "The Problem of Priests in the World." *Commonweal,* 82:105–9 (April 16, 1965).

Lehmann, K. "The Root of Priestly Office." *Theology Digest,* 18:228–36 (Fall, 1970).

Marsh, T. "Christian Priesthood." *Furrow,* 22:260–68 (May, 1971).

Milner, P. "The Question of Priesthood." *New Blackfriars,* 50:529–32 (July, 1969).

Milroy, D. "The Priest in the Modern World." *Tablet*, 225:175–76 (February 20, 1971).

Mohler, J. "The Priesthood of All Believers." *Homiletic & Pastoral Review*, 71:76–83 (August–September, 1971).

Mulligan, J. "The Priest as Revolutionary." *Homiletic & Pastoral Review*, 69:915–23 (September, 1969).

Myers, R. "Confusion Among Priests." *Homiletic & Pastoral Review*, 72:65–68 (December, 1971).

Nahmon, R. "I Am a Priest—What Am I?" *Homiletic & Pastoral Review*, 71:268–83 (January, 1971).

Nolan, J. "What Young People Think of Priests." *National Catholic Reporter*, 7:8 (October 15, 1971).

Nordhus, T. "Fuzzy Image." *Priest*, 27:58–62 (January, 1971).

O'Grady, J. "Personal Fulfillment for the Priest." *Priest*, 27:17–23 January, 1971).

O'Rourke, K. "Positive Options for Contemporary Ministry." *Priest*, 27:36–45 (January, 1972).

Padovano, A. "The Future of the Ministry." *National Catholic Reporter*, 7:9 (October 15, 1971).

Pepler, C. "State of the Priesthood." *Priest*, 27:75–77 (March, 1971).

Pohlschneider, J. "Le Prêtre au milieu des remous de notre époque." *Documentation catholique*, 69:969–76 (November 1, 1970).

"Le Prêtre en difficulté: symposium." *Le Supplément*, 95:395–432 (November, 1970).

"Priesthood: Function or State?" *Month*, 4:35–36 (August, 1971).

Quesnell, Q. "From New Testament Text to Priesthood Tomorrow." *Chicago Studies*, 10:187–200 (Summer, 1971).

Rahner, K. "The Consecration of the Layman to the Care of Souls." in *Theological Investigations*, London, Darton, Longman & Todd, 1961– , 3:263–76.

"The Position of Woman in the New Situation in Which the Church Finds Herself." Ibid., 8:75–93.

"Priest and Poet." Ibid., 3:294–317.

"Priestly Existence." Ibid., 3:239–62.

"Reflections on the Contemporary Intellectual Formation of

Future Priests." Ibid., 6:113–38.

"The Renewal of Priestly Ordination." Ibid., 3:171–76.

"The Sacramental Basis for the Role of the Layman in the Church." Ibid., 8:51–74.

"The Theology of the Restoration of the Diaconate." Ibid., 5:268–314.

Requier, C. "Priestly Moorings." *Priest,* 27:41–48 (June, 1971).

Riemslag, A. "Ministers of the Church." *American Ecclesiastical Review,* 165:105–13 (October, 1971).

Roquet, A.-M. "La Théologie du caractère et l'incorporation à l'église." *La Maison Dieu,* 32:74–89 (1952).

Schallert, E., and Kelley, J. "Some Factors Associated with Voluntary Withdrawal from the Catholic Priesthood." *Homiletic & Pastoral Review,* 71:95–106 (November, 1970); 177–83 (December, 1970); 254–67 (January, 1971).

Schillebeeckx, E. "Priesterschap." *Theologisch Woordenboek,* Roermond en Maaseik, Romen, 1958.

Schlichte, G. "The Vanishing Priest, a Sign from God to Change Our Ways?" *American Ecclesiastical Review,* 161:334–43 (November, 1969).

Schlier, H. "New Testament Elements of Priestly Office." *Theology Digest,* 18:11–18 (Spring, 1970).

Stuhlmueller, C. "The Priest in His Prophetic Role." *American Ecclesiastical Review,* 166:147–56 (March, 1972).

Sullivan, J. "The Priest as Prophet." *Homiletic & Pastoral Review,* 71:66–72 (May, 1971).

Swain, L. "Apostolate and Priesthood in the New Testament." *Clergy Review,* 55:679–91 (September, 1970).

Sweetser, T. "Personal and Sacramental Priesthood." *Cross & Crown,* 23:62–67 (March, 1971).

"Symposium on the Priesthood." *Worship,* 43:68–124 (February, 1969).

Synod of Bishops, Third International. "The Ministerial Priesthood." *Catholic Mind,* 70:33–51 (March, 1972).

Tkacik, A. "Priesthood, Prophecy and Wisdom in the Old Testament and Contemporary Church." *American Benedictine Review,* 21:507–25 (December, 1970).

Walter, J. "Priest or Minister?" *Month,* 4:110–14 (October, 1971).

Wuerl, D. "Priesthood and Witness." *Priest,* 27:18–21 (July–August, 1971).

　　"The Third Synod of Bishops on the Ministerial Priesthood." *Homiletic & Pastoral Review,* 72:48–56 (January, 1972).

Yzermans, V. A. "American Contributions to the Decree on the Ministry and Life of Priests." *American Ecclesiastical Review,* 155:145–63 (September, 1966).